Teera

A LIFE OF HOPE AND FULFILLMENT

Teera de Fonseka and Patrick Meissner

ISBN: 1502309599
ISBN 13: 9781502309594
Library of Congress Control Number: 2014916197
CreateSpace Independent Publishing Platform
North Charleston, South Carolina

DEDICATION

This book is dedicated to my dear children and
the generations to come. Also to the reader, in
the sincere hope that God will give you courage
and strength to move forward. I don't regret my
mistakes anymore, for I would not be where
I am today if not for them. I followed my heart.
I do not know any other way. I pray that you, too,
will live your life with no regrets.

INTRODUCTION

By: Teera de Fonseka

I am so thankful to my daughter, Shirlene, for making me write my story. Her ability to go with the flow, adjust to every situation, and get along with everyone is inspiring. She has always had the capacity to smile under any circumstance. I owe my children gratitude for their patience throughout the times when I was so lost, when I was battling to have a second chance for us to be together. Their re-assuring smiles gave me the courage it took to walk the desert for many years, and hold on to my child-like faith in God's plan.

My story is about a painful journey to freedom. God's amazing grace and mercy brought us to America. At the time I was willing to settle anywhere in the world to be able to live together with my children in peace. Never, in my wildest dreams, did I imagine that place would be the United States.

I am speaking from the perspective of my experiences; this is the story of only one woman, of many, in our vast world. We learn and grow from each other's stories. I cannot say I expect you to agree with everything I say. I only hope my comments and views may be useful to you.

Among the many lessons that I have learned, one is that freedom is a great privilege, and should never be taken for granted. I earned my freedom only through a lot of hard work and determination. I am willing to say definitively: the results are always worth it.

Writing my story gave me relief, release, and comfort. It also helped me to rebuild my life, regain my strength, and move past the pain. Most importantly, writing my story enabled me to learn my own strength.

I used my own name in this book; some names have been changed for the sake of privacy and protection, but all of the stories in this book are painstakingly real. I beat myself for a very long time for the mistakes I made. I tried so hard to find a reason for living, a reason for surviving. We do not know really what our true calling is, but I can tell you it is all about how we treat each other.

We can never know who will be a part of our journey, and when we will lose them, or when they will lose us. A part of the success of our life's journey consists of having good relationships with those who cross our path. This will require patience, sacrifice, and doing the best we can with the time we have available to us. We need to love, forgive, and endeavor to understand. We need to be thoughtful, generous and helpful. It is important to do this because when we reach the end of our journey, we can leave behind lasting memories and good examples for those who continue on their own journey.

It is our job to know who we are, what we value, and what we are supposed to be doing here. That's what success is. It is being at peace with the knowledge that you gave it your all. Sometimes we have to let go of our expectations so that we can be true to ourselves. That is probably the most difficult thing that anyone can do, but we must if we ever want to move forward.

My concept of God was that he was a punitive figure. I had confused Him with my early experiences of authority figures. When bad things happened and I was treated unjustly, I questioned God over and over. WHY? What did I do so wrong so that I would be punished so severely? Over time I learned that all things work together for good, for the person who loves God, and who is called according to God's purpose. I am blessed to have seen a silver lining of hope that has kept me moving forward, which is learning that God is my strength.

I had been devastated and experienced many disappointments and hurtful situations. It took many years to stop dwelling on the nasty scar on my face. There were times I wished I were a man so that I could grow a beard to cover it. Other times I wished to be old so the wrinkles would disguise it. I believed that was the only way I could fit in with normal society again.

The challenges I have undergone have been both physical and emotional. There were times when I was consumed with self-pity. I felt sorry for myself for having been used, abused, ridiculed scarred for life, and deceived so easily. I felt like a naive fool, where every tactic that was used on me worked. I experienced a terrible sense of isolation and am amazed that I did not explode on the spot.

It took so long for me to accept that the forces working for me were greater than the forces working against me. We need to choose our battles wisely. I remember how my outlook on life changed when I met the Good Shepherd sisters at the Welcome House. Those first days at the Welcome House, and the subsequent contacts and divine connections that occurred during my stay there, all come to my mind as I reflect and recount my past.

I genuinely try to understand life, all of life, not just my own. Through it all I never doubted my own ability to love. I only doubted, at times, that my love would be returned. I longed for someone and feared that they would never come. My neediness used to paralyze me with so much pain and lead me to many mistakes. Often I felt that I have suffered at least three times more than a normal person should in one lifetime. There were moments where I was at the depth of my sorrow, but the pains and the struggles helped me grow.

I may have forgotten the specifics of what certain people have said, and I may have forgotten some minor details about the events I shared with these people, but I will never forget how they made me feel. It feels like I am in a calm place after having battled heavy storms.

Now I know that peace truly begins with each of us being comfortable with who we are as a person.

It is amazing how a person can face so many tragedies and obstacles in one's life, and be able to survive and pick up the pieces. I wasted so much valuable time trying to convince the world of my innocence. At the same time I beat myself for my blind faith in people. I am so blessed to be able to convey my victories, my failures, and my victories that occurred in spite of my failures. No matter what we go through in life, we should never allow our hearts to become hardened. We should remind ourselves that Jesus came to serve and to save, not to judge or condemn.

You can tell a lot about people by the way they treat their servants. Love, forgiveness, generosity and gratitude are great blessings that can help you conquer adversity in your life. I made many poor choices, but I know my heart is right. We need to forgive others as well as ourselves. Resentment is a waste of time and energy. If we take the time to take the high road, to understand why people do what they do, forgiveness comes easily.

Now I think a lot about how everything that took place has affected the lives of the people around me, especially my children and my parents. They too felt pain and suffering. They too were left with scars. They too, have learned to be the bearer of hope for those who have been handed a bad deal.

It is a great feeling to see my children smile. Come to think of it, they have always managed to smile at any circumstance. Once I asked my children how they managed to smile. They all gave the same answer: "We blocked out our sad feelings," they said, "because we learned that was the only way."

By the time we reunited, my children were teenagers. You can tell your grown up children when you feel they have not acted properly, or you can be silent, let them see their own mistakes, and be there to lift them up if they fall, or fail. There is not a more reliable approach than love if we want to become all that we are meant to be. Love never fails.

Some people rush from one thing to the next, driven by ambition and the need to succeed. They have filled their lives with stress. We need to calm down and pay attention, or we may miss the best parts of living.

I have learned to appreciate the countless blessings that have been given to me and I am determined to go the extra mile to bring out the best in the people that have been put in my life. We may not realize it, but our ability to influence others may be stronger than we believe. We need to choose our words wisely, for sometimes the message sent might not be the message received.

What we do or say has an impact on the people around us. It is up to us to take the steps along the path that we want for ourselves and those we love. We need to surround ourselves with people that help bring us up.

I need to be a part of something where people care about one another, set high standards, and honor truth. I feel especially passionate about this, because my trust has been violated so many times before. My trust can only be given as a special gift. It takes strength for me to trust now, the kind of strength that is most hard to find.

No matter who we are, we have encountered obstacles and challenges in our lives. Some of us move on. No person is without conflict, whether it is tragedy, stormy relationships, challenges at work, or facing day to day obstacles in life. It is how we deal with conflict that determines who we are.

Writing, reading, listening and enduring pain teaches you a lot too. Faith in God and the faith in yourself that you will survive, play critical roles in life. You have to slow your life down to find out if you are actually living the life you are meant to live.

I never knew the importance of putting myself first, but you have to sometimes. I remember my psychiatrist, Dr. Pillai, once told me during a session, "Thea," he said. "You have to save yourself before you can try to save the world." He could never get my name right, but he certainly could read my mind. I didn't understand him at the time, but now that many years have passed, his caring words are more relevant to me than they ever had been.

Now I feel like I am a part of America. It is home and I love it here. It is a great place to mature. Most importantly, we need to learn that what is most valuable is not what we have in our possessions, but whom we have in our lives. It is so great to have well-intentioned people supporting us. We need to be prepared for what might happen, and prepare to embrace who we are. Only then will the doors open.

Final Thoughts:

I should be dead, and yet I am still here.

I have smiled through the flames of fire, and have led a good life. I have had both gratifying and disappointing experiences. The people who really matter to me looked past my scars and treated me with the utmost respect. They seemed to have noticed my strength more than I did.

These days, when I look in the mirror, I don't pay attention to the scars. I see a woman who has overcome and conquered. Lately I have come to accept that it is essential that my scar remains on my face, unhidden, as evidence of a life interrupted many times, and as a reminder to myself that looks have nothing to do with achievements. It was God within who carried me through the long desert and sent many great people along the path to give me hope during the times where it felt like I had reached a dead end.

I do not wish upon my enemies the trials I had to face in my lifetime. I still may not be what I ought to be, but I am not what I used to be. There was a time I wished to be anyone else – anyone – but today there is nobody that I would want to trade places with. Some of us are given a second chance, and there is no time for regrets. We should take one day at a time, learn that God is in control, and move on.

Often I thought my world would come to an end, and yet I am still here. I am constantly reminded that I had never been abandoned, even though, at times, it felt like I was. Now that I have overcome my brokenness and grief, regained my humanity, and most importantly, forgiven those who have hurt me, I feel it is my mission to spread the word of God through personal experiences and example.

It was January 26, 2014. Keeping my word is very important to me. That afternoon I was debating on making a crucial decision of having to compromise to keep my word. I was stressed, confused, and tremendously burdened when the phone rang. It was a friend. She said her 13-year-old daughter has learned two new songs and was waiting to sing them to me.

Instantly I stepped out and walked to their place to forget my problems. I wanted to encourage the kid who appreciates my approval and presence in her life. I consider myself honored and privileged that she does. Her name is Takisha.

She sang "You Raise Me Up" with her amazing and powerful voice. I have never heard a kid sing with such passion. She also sang the song "Amazing Grace." Tears of joy filled my eyes. The burden was lifted off me.

Sometimes God has a kid's voice. I got the answer I needed. Compromise was not an option. It is amazing how much we could learn from children if we give them the time of day. I love spending time with open-minded kids with positive energy and new ideas. They bring so much joy and quality to my life.

Miracles take place when we forget about our problems and focus on someone who needs our time and attention. And wow, the rewards are *awesome*. It is a tremendous relief to be able to trust in God, so that He can take the burden off your shoulder. Never give up hope. Miracles happen every day.

Teera

A LIFE OF HOPE AND FULFILLMENT

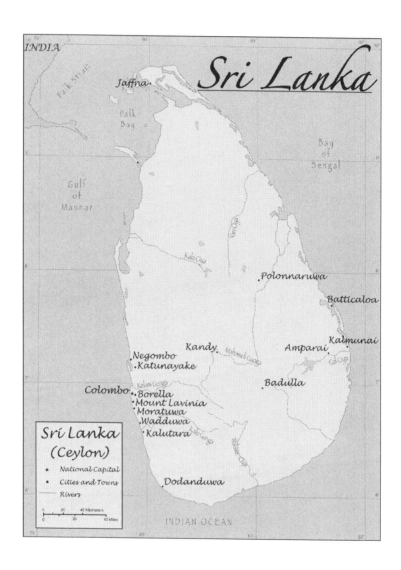

I

I had already packed my bag the night before, so it was easy for me to sneak out of my room before anyone woke up. Not that I needed to sneak out. For once, I wasn't hiding from anyone. I just didn't want to wake any of the other women as they peacefully slept. I'd be seeing them all soon enough anyways, and I had to catch a bus.

It was a little bit after 5 a.m. when I carefully stepped out into the dark hallway with brown plaster walls and three bedrooms on either side. I took one last look into my barren, little room with its empty dresser and stripped bed.

I hadn't done much to make that place my own. There was too much on my mind for the few years that I called that room in the Welcome House my home. Still, I couldn't help but feel as though I was leaving a part of me behind when I gently closed the thin, wooden door behind me.

The floorboards creaked beneath my feet as I made my way down the stairs. I stopped by the nursery where four tiny infants were sleeping in peace. From there I exited through the front office, out the door, and on to the verandah.

I stepped through the tall gates and into the bleary streets of Borella before sunrise. A few vendors slowly set up shop. Vagrants, awakened by the light of the sky, sat upright and still beneath their blankets, too sleepy to start the day. Sporadic voices echoed against the pavement and brick walls, a prelude to the rumble of conversation that would consume the streets as the day matured.

I must have been walking too slowly, because my bus almost left without me. I had to run after it and flag down the driver to let me in. Out of breath and now wide awake, I found a seat down the aisle and relaxed for a minute. It would be a long day of goodbyes for me, so I took a minute to relish the white noise of the bus engine. I felt like I was in a dream; I couldn't believe it was actually happening.

The sun had risen by the time the bus made its way nearly two hours from Borella to Moratuwa. The chill of the morning had left the air. Warm sunlight pressed against my skin as I set foot down the road. Past rows of neatly lined, single story, stone houses, I arrived at the home where my parents were living at the time.

I could tell the house was crowded as my steady, confident steps drew me nearer. My brother's cars were parked outside, and bodies moved quickly back and forth in the windows that peered into the kitchen. There was a murmur of muffled voices and a steady stirring that could be heard from behind the door.

Excited, and yet still hesitant, I braced myself for all of the attention I was about to receive, took a deep breath, and turned the front doorknob. As it opened, the sound became clear and more voluminous. By the time I was able to get both feet over the threshold, the calamity suddenly stopped. There was a quiet pause while more than fifteen eager faces met mine, inhaled, and contemplated what to say next.

"Hello everyone!" I said with glee, breaking the silence.

The room burst back into chaos, the sound even louder than it was before. There was not a single living member of my extended family, on the island of Sri Lanka, that was not at my parents' house that morning. They had come from destinations both far and near to see me off.

We had some time to relax before leaving for Novena and eventually, the airport. I took a minute to go through the pile of items stacked in my parents' room. There were of course the clothes and personal items that I had packed a few days before: a gold bangle that my mamma had bought me when I was a little girl, a picture of Chandra, and pictures of my children.

I really didn't have much to bring. The bulk of the heavy stack of boxes and bags that I brought with me were from my family and bound for my brother Cyril. It was expensive to ship him care packages all the way to the U.S., so my siblings and parents figured it would be cheaper to pack their gestures in with my luggage.

Satisfied that everything was accounted for, I zipped up my bag and gave myself one quick look in the mirror. I thought about how much my face had changed over the past 12 years. I looked healthy. I had a full head of hair. I was eating right, and for the most part, sleeping well.

I put a little make-up on the scar above my lip, but not much. Over the years it had blended in with the skin on my face, but you could still see it. Plastic surgery could only do so much, and makeup could only soften the line. It hung beneath my nose and extended in either direction across both cheeks; like a permanent, dark frown that's still visible, even when I'm smiling. It was a reminder of the night that got me into this whole mess in the first place.

When the time came, we all piled into a caravan of cars and headed to Borella, where I had started my day, for the afternoon Novena at the All Saints Church. I was so thankful and so excited it was hard to focus on praying. It was just bliss. All I could think was, "Thank You."

After the service, the crowd of family that I came with made small talk in front of the church and slowly inched to their cars. The All Saints Church was about two hundred yards from the Welcome House, and just like I planned, there was more than enough time to stroll back over there and say my goodbyes.

The street was buzzing now that the day had pressed on. The quiet vendors from the morning were now busily trading their wares and haggling with customers. The homeless who camped in the alleys had packed up their coir mats and blankets, headed elsewhere for the day. I inhaled deep as I ambled down the side of the road toward the convent where I found Sister Finbarr waiting for me outside the gates.

She was beaming, smiling like I had never seen her before. The two of us embraced and gently let go. We were both so proud of each other, and so happy to be at the end of this long, painful road. Sister Finbarr put her arm around my shoulder and led me through the gates, just like she did the first time we met.

"Teera," she said as we stepped down the dusty, dirt driveway, toward the convent. "I don't want you to take this the wrong way, but I am so happy to see you leave."

She already knew that she wasn't going to offend me. We both smiled.

"You've grown up so much since you came here," she went on. "I still remember when that," she paused to find the right word, "when that…man…first sent you here."

I chuckled at how delicately she described him. "I remember that too," I said. "I remember feeling so relieved! It was the first time I had felt safe in so long."

"And I remember thinking that you could still save your marriage!"

"Sister, you don't have to…"

"But I do." It wasn't the first time she had brought up this conversation. "I still can't forgive myself for not seeing what he was doing to you."

"It's OK," I said. "You found out soon enough, right?"

"I just wish it could have been sooner."

"I just wish I didn't have to leave," I changed the subject.

"Me either, Teera. But like I said, I'm so happy to see you go."

We stepped through the waiting room and into the counseling room, a plain space with wooden chairs, white plaster walls, and a few tables. It was mostly used for group sessions, and even though it did not seem like a very inviting room, there were miracles that happened in that place.

A few of my friends were already waiting for me so they could say their goodbyes. You could hear footsteps through the ceiling and down the wooden stairs as the room began filling with the women that I had grown so close to. They were the women that helped save my life. There were tears and stories, hugs and goodbyes. Sister Bernadette couldn't stop smiling. She told me to send something good like an alarm clock when I got there.

When it was time to leave, Sister Finbarr walked me back down the front steps of the convent. The twenty or so women that made up the Welcome House surrounded us as we embraced one last time.

"You're going to do great," she said. "Don't you worry for a minute, Teera, God will be with you, always."

I couldn't find the words, other than to just tell her that I would miss her, that I would miss everyone. It was hard to articulate just how grateful I was to all of them. When we finally let each other go, I continued back down the driveway and stepped into my brother's car.

My family had parked their cars outside of the gates of the Welcome House in a long caravan. They had pulled up after they left church, and were waiting for me to finish saying my goodbyes. When I was ready to get rolling, all seven or so cars started on their way with us to the airport in Katunayake. It was a two-hour drive at best.

It was well after sunset by the time we all made it to the airport. My family followed me through the terminal like they were my entourage. They walked me to the busy gate where security would not let them proceed any further. It was time for my last set of goodbyes, and I knew that this one would be the hardest.

I remember seeing the hope in my children's faces and the concern in my mother's. She looked on with sadness, not fully convinced that she was ready to let go of her youngest daughter.

It was then that Marcus reminded my mother that, "tonight we can sleep peacefully knowing that Maxie can't hurt her anymore. She's going to be OK," he said, trying to make light of the situation. "She's going to be with family as soon as she gets off her flight. We've done everything we can to keep Bubby safe here. You can let the Mother of Sorrows go, mamma! Things are going to be much more peaceful for all of us!" Marcus' playful smile slowly disappeared when he took in the gravity of his own words.

You could see my mother swell with courage when he said it. She approached me, her eyes welling, and took out the gold bangle she was wearing for the special occasion. She held it out in her hand and gave it to me as a keepsake. My mother speculated that this would be the last time that the two of us saw each other. I didn't want to believe her then, but it turned out that she was right.

After having said my final goodbyes, I stepped timidly through the airport terminal inching closer towards a new life for myself. Each step was a bittersweet leap of hope and achievement. After so many years of praying for some sort of reprieve from my misery, the day had actually come. The stale air of that never-ending plane ride was like an unfamiliar, yet charmingly welcome purgatory to what I knew would be better days.

Sri Lanka was not always a place to escape from. In many ways, I wish I never had to leave. But I did, and that's a long story that I'm only beginning to address. When I was growing up, Sri Lanka was paradise. It was home, and I didn't know anything outside of the little teardrop shaped island off the coast of India that we called Ceylon.

I was raised in a small village called Wadduwa located on the southern shore of Sri Lanka, not too far from the capital in Colombo. Nestled close to the beach, in the staggering humidity of a tropical village, it was a beautiful place to grow up. On most days the town was vibrant with the endearing humility of good people who knew very little beyond the simplicity of village life. As a little girl, it was the perfect place to stretch my legs and test my imagination.

Wadduwa was a refuge for my parents and my older siblings. They had escaped from Colombo during the Easter Sunday Raid in 1942. Fleeing for their lives following an Easter breakfast disrupted by bomb blasts from Japanese Zeros, they took what little they could bring and settled in a warm cottage near a beach lined with coconut trees.

It is customary where I come from to name the home that your family resides in. A lot of families would proudly display the name of their first-born son somewhere near the door. Others would display religious tributes or anything else that might be relevant to their household. My family's home had a wooden sign with the name "Sea Breeze" carved into it, a tribute to both the ocean we lived on, and the safe serenity that home granted our family.

I was born a little more than a year later, in November of 1943, the youngest of ten siblings. My family lovingly referred to me by my nickname 'Bubby.' It was an endearing term that has stuck with me my whole life. The title Bubby became more than just a name; it was a symbol of my place in the family, and in many ways my place in the world.

So long as I was 'Bubby,' there was always an older sibling or a parent looking after me, and they usually had a good reason to. I had a habit of finding myself in compromising circumstances. I was constantly getting myself into trouble, or at least that was the way that my family saw it. As such, I spent much of my childhood trying to evade the notion that I was the younger sibling that required special attention. Yet, despite my best efforts, I remained 'Bubby,' the one my family looked out for, even into my older years.

By the time I was old enough to remember anything, my two eldest brothers, Cyril and Titus, had joined the Royal Navy and left home to serve. Another one of my brothers, Theobalt, had passed away in infancy. I was named Theodora after him. I never really liked that name so I always went by Teera.

For most of my life, there were seven children, including myself, plus my parents, crammed into our tiny cottage by the beach. It was chaotic, to say the least. Each child was in a different phase of life, so each child had his or her own obsessions and respective levels of maturity.

For example, my sisters Juliet and Sheila were older and had always looked after me. But then there was my sister Margaret, who was only a few years older than I. Because Margaret and I were so close in age, we found that the two of us could confide in each other as we were growing up.

Margaret and I were the last two left when everyone else had moved on. Margaret would often take care of me. She combed and braided my hair before we would leave for school. She helped me study for my senior exams and bought me beautiful clothes when she started working and making a little money.

In the evenings my pappa would share a drink with my mamma. After a few he would often turn to her and say, "You know, Victa, we are a very special couple."

"Is that so?" she'd reply coyly, having heard this one before. "How is it that we are a very special couple?"

"Good question, Victa!" he'd say. "We are a very special couple, because you and I have royal names! Named after his and her highnesses themselves, Queen Victoria and King Charles!"

He became enamored with the idea that the two of them had the same names as English royalty when Queen

Elizabeth visited Sri Lanka in 1954, following her crowning. The whole island celebrated the visit when it happened. But my father was one of the few people that talked about it for years to come. He didn't care that both King Charles and Queen Victoria had died decades ago, or that Prince Charles was only a baby at the time. My mamma and my poppa had royal names, and Poppa was proud of that.

My father was unique. An architect by trade, he had retired from government work and was working independently by the time I was born. He kept an office in a spare bedroom in our cottage that was completely off limits to the rest of the family. Inside was his drawing board and his tools, pictures of his family and religious trinkets that he had accumulated over the years. I'd often see him pouring over blueprints late into the night; so focused and silent, relaxed even.

He was tough and stern, yet gentle and heroic. He was someone to be afraid of, but also someone to confide in. My father loved his children and his daughters had a special place in his heart.

"God help the man that would try to hurt any of you," he would say. I would have to wait until I was a teenager to learn just how serious a statement that was.

Pappa's prized possession was his authentic Honda motorcycle. It was one of five genuine Honda bikes on the whole island of Sri Lanka, and somehow he managed to get his hands on one. More than a convenient way to get to job sites, Pappa's motorcycle really meant something to him. It was his way of hiding his soft side, so that he could still feel mean, without actually being mean.

Naturally he would want to keep the bike safe from rain and thieves, so he parked it in the living room. My sisters and I were always embarrassed when we had to explain to visitors why our living room had a dirt bike in it. Most guests figured we were strange to begin with. They shrugged it off as something they probably should have expected.

For a while, my sisters and I tried to keep the room clean when it was not being used as a garage. We eventually had to give up on it. No matter how hard we worked to scrub that floor, Pappa would burst in through the front door every evening with his filthy tires spraying mud and exhaust everywhere.

In many ways, my mother was a perfect complement to my father. He was bombastic. My mother, on the other hand, was graceful. Generous and gentle, she was sharp as a tack, but would never let you know it. Her voice was beautiful, even though she sang rarely. She swam like a dolphin and remained one of the more beautiful women in Wadduwa, even after birthing 10 children. Before she became consumed with her duties as a mother, she ran a successful rickshaw business. My father was a very lucky man, and he knew it.

Mamma looked after the affairs of the household. She ran a tight ship, and all of us children had the utmost respect for her wishes. Pappa supplied the income, and it was her duty to stretch the scant resources she had to make sure that every one of us ate and stayed healthy.

She drove a particularly hard bargain when it came to buying groceries, particularly fish. She knew how the fish salesmen worked their business and spent a lifetime learning every trick of the trade. She had an eyeball for the weight of a fish and could always spot when someone was embellishing. She always remembered to look down the fish's throat to make sure it had not been stuffed with sand to bulk up the weight and price.

She had a stone cold stare and would never budge, often angering vendors with her tactics. If she didn't get the price she wanted, she would simply walk away until the seller came calling back for her saying, "for *you*, ma'am, I'll make an exception."

She found ways to make fish and rice last for meals on end. She was creative and shrewd and never considered herself to be her first priority. Whatever extra money mamma had, she saved for her daughters' dowries.

During each meal, she would fix a plate of food for an elderly woman, suffering from tuberculosis, who lived on the other side of our town. My brothers always tried to eat the extra plate, but mamma insisted that it was more important to share what you have, even if what you have is very little.

The days we had off from school we would often go to the beach and watch the fishermen work. Watching the fishermen was always a scene. They gathered their equipment and prepared nets throughout the day before setting off on voyages in the evening. In the morning a crew would arrive from the previous night's work to be greeted by a throng of helping hands waiting for them on the beach.

Helpers gathered to painstakingly drag each massive net loaded with waterlogged and still flapping fish. If the catch that day was good the excitement was contagious because it meant full bellies and busy markets. They'd tread through waist-deep water singing, "Odi! Ellai! Ellia! Odi! Ellai! Ellia!" over and over again until every last net was brought to shore.

Fish jumped out of the nets as they were dragged through the sand, creating a faint trail of squirming mackerel all the way to the cutting tables. It was a competition amongst the young children to see how many loose fish they could collect.

The game was all about speed and the kids who lived on the beach would get mad because I ran faster than they could. "Get your own fish!" they'd yell as I came whizzing by. It was a lot of fun if you didn't mind getting scales and fish slime all over your arms.

Our biggest competitors were the birds as they came to pick at the slowly breathing guppies flopping through the sand. They'd scatter all around us as we ran, creating a torrent of feathers and squawking, but most of the time my basket was full before they had a chance to peck at my collection. Then, it was back to home to dump my fishy basket on the kitchen table, and then back to the beach for more.

While the fish were being unloaded and prepared, the fishmongers were waiting with baskets strapped to their backs or wraps around their shoulders. When the first fish made it past the cutting tables a wave of raised voices would descend on the deck hands scrambling to get their hands on the best catch at the best price. Those who were quick would escape through the wall of salesmen with a full basket, chanting, "Fiiish! Fiiiiish!" They would circle through the rows of homes, as women would come from their doors to bargain for a cheaper price on what would become that night's dinner.

By the end of the day, the fishmongers would take what they had left and catch the late train to strike business in more remote areas. You could smell them from three compartments over, if you didn't already hear their voices echoing on the platform. They were foul smelling and foul speaking; shouting profanities across train compartments that were so packed with people you could hardly put your feet down.

Our family attended Sunday mass at the church of the Holy Sprit. Of course, back then, service was always chanted in Latin. We never missed Sunday Mass, and pappa always made sure the family was up early enough to walk there. He'd pester us until we were ready to file out the door. Then he'd hop on his motorcycle, start up the engine and haul off without us.

We didn't mind walking. We all knew that pappa just wanted to show off his bike when he got to mass. It was one of his many quirks, and something that we found to be endearing. There was nothing intimidating about the way he rode his bike, even though he carried himself like he was the roughest, meanest biker Wadduwa had ever known.

He rolled along at a slow roar, putt-putting through potholes and bumps, never taking the bike out of first gear. We used to joke that you could read a book while riding on the back. Far from exciting or dangerous, he was a definite nuisance to peaceful churchgoers as he parked his rumbling motorcycle in front of the church doors.

We were loud when we got to mass. It wasn't just my pappa's motorcycle; we were all loud. There were so many of us, it was hard not to be loud. People stared when we entered the church. They whispered amongst themselves and acted as if we were spoiling the morning for everyone else. I understood how annoying we might have been with all of our noise and dust. But then again, all that we brought with us was noise and dust.

There was no need for the rest of the church to judge us like they did, but that's the way it was. If you missed mass, it was a sin. If you disrespect God, he will punish you. If you disturb the sanctity of this town's church on Sunday, you won't be welcome back. I never understood the idea of pre-judging one's fate in the afterlife, but it seemed many people in our parish were already certain of who was on Saint Peter's list, and who still hadn't made the cut.

I was always under the impression that everyone would go to heaven. I couldn't understand how God could cast out one of his own creations. What I did understand, however, was the difference between right and wrong. As far as I'm concerned, we were not doing anything wrong. Still, even in the sanctity of that church, there was no way to escape the feeling of a finger being pointed your way. It was the feeling of unmerited condemnation, and it was something that I was going to have to get used to.

II

Step, step. Step, step. Step, step. Step, step. The pace quickens as my breaths become shorter. Step, step. Step, step. Step, step. Step, step. I think I'm ahead, I think I'm safe, but I can't look back. Step, step. Keep focused on the ground in front of you. Step, step. You can see the end, Teera. Step, step. And you can't see the others, they must be behind you. Step, step. Lean into it, you're almost there. Step, step, lunge! A deep roar emerges from the crowd to my right. Step, step. Step, step. My pace slows. I relax my wildly swinging legs so that I can stop their motion and keep my balance. My lungs stretch and grasp at the dusty air kicked up by the defeated behind me.

I strained my eyes to pick their faces out of the crowd. It didn't take long to find the familiar smile of my father as he bounced up and down in the small expanse of heads shouting, "way to go Bubby! That's my little girl!"

By his side, my mother beamed with pride and chuckled at his enthusiasm. It was the second time I had won the senior champion cup at the Good Shepherd Convent. After many months of training, all my hard work had finally paid off. I took that trophy home and placed it on my dresser, right next to the one I had received the year before. "Maybe I can start a collection," I thought to myself as I caught my reflection in the pale glint of the plastic, gold painted sculpture of a sprinter at mid-stride.

I always loved running. It was my favorite thing to do when I was younger. It was all I thought about when I was in school. In the morning I'd run to my classes; in the afternoon, I'd run all the way home. If the teacher ever needed a note or a book delivered to another class, she'd come right to me and I'd take off like a screaming banshee, sprinting from door to door in record time.

Winning that cup was a proud moment for me. Running was what defined me in those days. In my family, particularly, I was the only person that took athletics seriously. Running was what I did best, and it became something I would carry with me for my whole life.

So many years later and my soul is still poised. My eyes are focused straight ahead and my intention leans boldly into the future. I've come a long way on this marathon that I began running decades ago. My bones constantly yearn for motion, for action. So many years later and I still want to grasp my days and wring out their essence for all that they are worth. I want to make a difference. I want to share the love that I have been given. I want to keep running for the rest of my life.

As I became older, my emotions matured, as did my physical appearance. I never considered myself to be especially beautiful, but there were definitely things about me that for one reason or another boys found appealing. It wasn't until my preteen years that I began to notice suggestive stares from the young men I came into contact with. The attention was a welcome indication that I wasn't anyone's little girl anymore. I was becoming an attractive young woman with new strengths and new fears, that at the time I was not yet familiar with.

My first taste of romance was a passionate pre-teen relationship with a boy named Sam from town. It was an intense case of young love. I was fourteen at the time and we dated for about a year. Sam was so cordial, polite and fun. I just loved being around him.

My father, however, didn't seem to share my enthusiasm when he found out about the two of us. The idea of his little girl dating was already enough for him to handle. But the bigger issue for him was the fact that Sam's family came from a lower caste than we did. Fearing potential embarrassment for our family, my father concluded that it would be best if he put an end to our relationship.

Rather than forbid Sam and me from seeing each other, my pappa's solution was to tell me to pack my bags. I tried to plead with him, but it was no use. His mind was made up and before I knew it, I was in the backseat of a car, with my sister and her new husband, driving nearly thirteen hours to go live with them in Amparai. According to Pappa's plan, I would finish school there, and return home "when I was ready."

Of course the idea of leaving all of my friends, of leaving Sam, was devastating. Pappa thought nothing of how hard it would be for me to uproot myself. I had to leave my friends, my family, my home, and the first boy that I ever had feelings for. It was hard to put all that behind me, just as hard as it was for me to understand why my father was making me do this.

I remember being so irritated as we pulled up the driveway that day. I wasn't paying attention to the new town I had come to, or my sister's street, or even the house I was going to be living in. The only thing I could think about was Sam, and how I never got a chance to say goodbye to him. I wanted to, but pappa wouldn't let me.

"You're lucky my baby hasn't come yet," Sheila broke in on my ruminations while helping me carry my luggage into the house. "I made a bed for you in the nursery. You can stay there until,"

"Until the baby comes? And then what? A mat?" I didn't mean to be that short with her. I was just having a lot of trouble being polite that day.

"We'll just have to see," Sheila said. "Who knows, by then Pappa might have forgotten all about this. You might be home by then!"

I didn't believe a word of it, but I could appreciate that my sister was just trying to raise my spirits. It was a tall task, and I wasn't going to make it easier on her. But Sheila tried because she was my big sister, and a good one at that. She figured that pleading with father would be a practice in futility.

She was probably on his side anyways. Rather than debating the issue, Sheila encouraged me to move on, to grow up and be strong. She tried to make light of the situation whenever possible, especially that day. Not to belittle my problems, but to teach me how to get past them. I never grew to call that place my home, but with her help, it stung a lot less to be there.

The first night I stayed there, Sheila cooked a big meal to make sure that I felt welcome. The look and smell of her recipes resembled my mother's, but you could tell that she was still missing a few of her finer points. She fried fish and made rice with curry, her pans greased with coconut oil. But the proportions were off. The textures were different even though the food smelled and looked about the same. It was mamma's cooking but not quite. It just made me miss home.

Sheila was just asking about the food when the front door opened, breaking our conversation.

"Sheila!" the light baritone of a short man echoed from down the hall.

"Hey, honey!" Sheila called back. "Dinner's ready! Come sit down,"

The man put down his hat and entered with arms outstretched. "Teera!" he said. "Welcome! I'm so glad you're staying with us!"

"Hi Dasa!" I said.

"Now Dasa," Sheila butted in, "remember, we didn't want Teera to come, and neither did she."

"I know!" Dasa took the severity out of the air, "but we're glad to see her just the same, right?"

"Right!" I jumped in hoping to change the subject.

"Dasa, let me get you a plate," Sheila seemed to read my mind. "I hope you're hungry, I made enough food to feed an army!"

Sheila put a plate on the table and the three of us sat back down to our meal. Dasa sat across from me, and we exchanged small talk. I sat next to him on the ride from Wadduwa to Amparai but beyond that, I had spent very little time with Sheila's husband. The two were married quickly and had moved from Wadduwa after the wedding.

He seemed a decent man and an adoring husband. The three of us all got along from the start. Even though it was never my choice to come to Amparai, it was still a good chance to become closer with the two of them. After Sheila had her baby, I knew that everything was going to be different between her and me.

As I quietly made my adjustment to life in Amparai, I learned that filling my time with countless distractions was a sure way to halt my feelings of loneliness. In the afternoons I would ferociously ride my bike home to get the rush of the wind in my hair. It was my little way of blowing off some steam every afternoon.

When the school day wound down I was restless in class, counting the minutes until I could hop on my bike and rush through the streets as fast as my legs would let me. Every day I passed by the police station and they soon caught on to my routine. They would yell "way to go,

Cycle Hero!" in Sinhala as I passed. I never broke stride. Whenever they yelled, I stood up on my bike to gain a quick boost of speed and show off how fast I could go.

I went to a government school in Amparai that was co-ed. I joined the track team, and when the coach realized that the other girls couldn't keep up with me, I started practicing with the boys' team. Some of them took it pretty hard when they learned that I was faster than them too. One boy even tried to tackle me in one of our races because I was beating him by a small gap. He missed me, and fell to the ground while I ran on and won the race.

It took a little getting used to, but I found myself feeling happy in Amparai. I liked my school, and I loved running for the track team. Sheila and I grew closer than we ever had been in the past. We spent our free time swapping stories and attending to the house. I kept myself busy enough to stop thinking about all my friends back home.

I was comfortable. Everything felt comfortable. Except, maybe, for my relationship with Dasa. I didn't feel like he was trying to make me uncomfortable, but he was. Every time he came home he would give me an unnecessarily long hug. The first time he did it, I thought he was just being affectionate. But he would follow the hug with suggestive eyes as he asked prodding questions about my day. I initially wrote off these advances as part of his character and tried not to let them bother me. But they didn't stop, and after a while, the way that Dasa treated me just felt wrong.

I didn't know what to do about it. I most definitely could not tell Sheila, I didn't have any proof that he actually had his eye on me. Even if I could prove it, I didn't want to potentially hurt or embarrass my sister. There was no use telling any of my friends from school; none of them knew me well enough to care.

I was right to have my suspicions about the man. One day I went to my room to change my clothes after school. I noticed noises coming from behind my closet door. The sound of shifting feet and heavy breathing startled me. I shrieked and backed away. The door burst open and Dasa emerged with ravenous eyes, slowly approaching me with his arms stretched open.

"I'm sorry Teera, did I scare you? I didn't mean to scare you. I'm sorry if I scared you," he whispered as he pulled me in by the arms and began kissing me. The scratch of his whiskers sent shivers down my spine. I stood as tense as I possibly could and stared straight forward as he moved in to kiss me on the lips.

I didn't know how to get away, I was disgusted, I wanted to vomit. I pretended as though I was calm and he eventually loosened his grip. Once he let go, I quietly slipped away to wash my mouth out in the sink.

When I returned to the room, I stood in the doorframe and stared at him. I didn't know if I should run. Where would I run? He didn't say anything but rather marched towards me, reared his arm up and back handed me hard enough that I fell to the ground beneath his feet.

When I got up to run, he grabbed me by the arm, dragged me back my room and locked the door behind me. I fell when he pushed me back in the room, and cowered in a ball on the cement floor. I could hear his footsteps march through the kitchen and out the front entry slamming the door behind him.

Hours had passed before I eventually heard the front door open again. The footsteps that walked in the house had a slow rhythm to them and I listened closely as they crept toward to the closet door. The hinges slowly creaked and the door opened revealing Dasa bearing an expression of fear and impending apologies.

He slowly crouched down, looked me in the eyes and said, "Teera, I am very sorry for doing this to you, but you have to promise me that you won't tell Sheila. I'll make it up to you, I swear, you just can't tell your sister."

I wanted to say something but remained silent to avoid provoking him. He took my silence as a sign that I would eventually tell my sister, and he was right. He kept pleading with me, as he knew this one incident might end his marriage.

"Please Teera, you can't tell Sheila!" he begged. "You know you don't want to. You know she would never understand. You don't want to put her through this, do you? Not while she's pregnant! Not while we have a baby on the way!"

It made me sick when he said it, because he made a very good point. I knew I would have to tell her eventually, but not now, not while she needed her husband and me. I silently nodded, and Dasa gratefully took that as his sign that he was off the hook. He left me a small gift, wrapped in a box, so that he could somehow make up for what he had just done to me. I left it on the floor and later tossed it deep in the garbage so that he wouldn't see.

After the incident I tried to maintain a sense of normalcy, avoiding contact with him whenever possible, but the advances wouldn't stop. Dinners were nauseating as I tried to work up an appetite with him eyeing me from across the table. He kept trying to pry into my social life, asking me about which boys I was going to be seeing. He even forbade me from seeing certain people in the vain hope that somehow I might give up and find him appealing.

I finally couldn't take it anymore and told Sheila everything while Dasa was at work one day. It broke my heart but I had to tell her. I didn't feel safe in that house with him. Sheila didn't know what to say. I asked her for forgiveness, but she wouldn't let me apologize. Instead she sent me to see my friends and waited for her husband to return home from work.

The air was thick when I came back that evening. For the first time, Dasa could not look *me* in the eyes. I quietly went to my room and waited for the night to pass. I could hear muffled shouting coming through the walls. I tried to sleep, but instead kept on replaying the events in my head. Eventually morning came and all I felt was guilt as I arose to a freshly broken household.

For the next few weeks I watched as the two of them attempted to live peacefully. Sheila, now in her third trimester, struggled to keep her composure. She wanted to seem as though the situation was not affecting her. But you could see the stress compounding on her face.

After she had her child, Sheila arranged for me to be sent back home. I wanted to stay and help her with the baby, but we both knew that it was best I leave. It was not an exciting homecoming knowing that I would be living with my father again, but that didn't make me any less glad to be there. I was home, and at least for a moment, things made sense again.

I started going to polytechnic school soon after my return. It was a much-needed distraction and a way of starting fresh. I had to take the train to get to school everyday, which put me at a healthy distance from my parents. Even though I was still living under their roof, the ability to be away from them for the majority of the day was liberating.

I made a few friends that were a lot more social than I was. They didn't have any problems disobeying their parents, or staying out past their curfews. I, still being very naïve and timid, found it hard to keep up. I didn't want to upset my parents, but I also wanted to stay out late and socialize. I wanted to meet boys and I wanted to have fun.

There was a shadow that hung over me when I initially got back from Amparai. I never had a chance to address the emotion when I was still living there. It was too uncomfortable living in that house with Dasa, but I felt it there too. It was the feeling of having been violated. I felt as though I wasn't safe in my own bed, and I felt it constantly.

After a few weeks of being back at school, I was well on my way to having healed from being molested by my brother-in-law. My new friends helped me gain back my confidence. Before I knew it, I just felt like Teera again.

One of my friends, Megan, had decided to elope with her boyfriend without her parents knowing. It was a bold move, and something that I personally would never have been capable of. Excited for my friend and excited for the party, I teamed up with some of the other girls from school and we put together a secret celebration. Megan's parents had no idea that she was going to be married, so we all had to make sure that they wouldn't find out.

The ceremony was held in the morning, on a weekday, so that we could act as though we were going to class when we were actually en route to the wedding. Everyone changed into party clothes when they got off the train and snuck off to the ceremony where we let down our guard and spent the morning celebrating.

When the wedding ended in the afternoon, the party moved down the street to the movie theater, but I had to change out of my party clothes and make my way home. I wanted to get back before my parents got worried.

I spent some time at the reception with a man that worked at the train station, named Norman. Norman was older, in his forties, and my friends and I would see him every morning as he attended to business at the station.

We all respected Norman because he was so much older and after so many mornings of seeing us off to school on time, he became a good friend and someone we trusted. He appeared as though he was the perfect gentleman when he offered to drive me back to his sister's house, so that I would have a place to freshen up before going home.

On our way there, he fumbled with small talk, attempting to keep me entertained. I would have gone to the movies with my friends, but I was insistent on getting back home before my parents found out that I had skipped school.

My plan appeared as though it was going to work out, except that when we got to Norman's sister's house, I found the place to be alarmingly empty. He led me to a room in the back where he shut the door, told me to change, and refused to leave.

"Go ahead, you can take off your clothes, it's ok, there's no one around," he said as I slowly began to back away from him.

"Come on, Teera," he said, "I thought that's what you came here for. Let me take your blouse off."

I thought about screaming but my throat choked up. I was trapped. I made a break for the door but Norman grabbed my arm and looked menacingly into my eyes.

"Where're you going, Teera? Don't you want to stay here a while?" he said.

He craned his neck to try and fit his mouth around mine. I struggled to break away but he tightened his grip, and threw me on the bed. Norman hastily knelt next to me and covered my mouth with his palm. My stuck throat suddenly loosened and I screamed into his hand. I bit into his finger, he let go and I managed a full volume scream. Norman wrapped his palm over my face. "Shut up!" he said as his eyes widened.

I fell back under the weight of his body and tried to picture something, anything that could take me away from that wretched moment in time. I thought of home and prayed for it to end. Minutes passed like days. My vision slowly blurred and my body went numb. I watched Norman have his way with me as I whimpered helplessly below him.

The earth was spinning when he finally let me walk away. The humanity, it seemed, had been stolen from me. Like he had taken my very soul and left behind nothing more than the fragile shell of a lifeless body. Broken and violated, I choked on a lump in my throat and shamefully put my clothes back on. Too frightened to leave and run away, I finally gave in, fell back on the bed and wept. Through thick tears I choked out a few quiet prayers, begging God for help.

I stayed the evening at Norman's, quietly coming up with reasons why all of this was my fault. I wanted to go home but there was no way I could face my parents that night. I could have made a break for the door but where was I going to go? I hadn't a clue where I was. With no other option, I remained motionless and contemplated what to do next.

It wasn't just that I was worried for my own safety. I was terrified of the condemnation that I knew would follow me in the weeks and months to come. In the culture that I came from, rape was almost always regarded as the woman's fault. My lack of willingness in the matter meant nothing, and this event would no doubt be regarded as the result of my promiscuity and nothing else. I imagined a future of endless persecution and fruitless attempts at finding a good man to start a family with.

My thoughts raced but came to a halt when Norman slowly put his chin on the back of my shoulder. He wanted to know why I was crying. Why was I crying? I choked at the audacity of his question. When I caught my breath, I mustered the strength to speak the last words that I would say to him that evening.

"How is anyone ever going to want to marry me now?" I said.

Norman's tone became aggressive. "What do you mean?" he said. "You don't want to be with me?"

I stared straight forward while he tried to reason with me, "but I love you," he said. "I want to marry you." It was more of a demand than a question, but I didn't know what to say, so I didn't say anything.

"We'll take the early train tomorrow. I want to meet your parents, and tell them the happy news. I'm not letting you go home unless you agree to let me go with you."

I nodded my head silently as he smiled and left the back of my shoulder.

Mamma and Pappa had apparently panicked the night before and went on a full-scale manhunt throughout every corner of town they could think of. When morning drew near they had assumed the worst, and with few places to look, arrived early at the train station to see if I had simply taken the morning train.

To their relief I had, in fact, taken the morning train. What they did not expect was for me to exit the train compartment with an older man named Norman on my shoulder. My father stared with disbelief when I broke the news that we were in love and would be married soon. I could tell in Mamma's eyes that she knew it was a lie. Pappa stared back as if he had just been informed that his daughter had died.

Pappa quietly held back his anger and accepted the news, feigning respect towards Norman. You could tell he didn't like the man. That night pappa tried to convince me that I was too young, but my mind had been made up. The decision to marry Norman, to me, seemed like my best, and in many ways, my only option.

But Pappa wasn't satisfied, and the next morning went about town inquiring as to where exactly this

Norman character had come from. Pappa had a reputation around town and kept up with friends in both high and low places. He reached out to all of them and before long, had found the answers that he was looking for.

When I returned home that afternoon, he was waiting for me with an older woman, slightly younger than my mother, with her daughter who was my age. When I opened the door, the woman met my eyes with a deep look of compassion, as if she knew without me telling her, everything that I was going through.

The daughter's head hung. She stared at the ground, withdrawn from the conversation. Father calmly, yet authoritatively instructed me to sit down and asked, "Bubby, do you know either of them?"

"No," I said, "I don't."

"Well then, would you like to introduce yourself?" Father invited and nodded knowingly at the woman.

"I don't know how to say this, Teera," the woman said, "but I am Norman's ex-wife. My name is Diane, and this is my daughter, Shelly. Your father told me that you two are to be married," she paused to reassure me that she was a friend before she went on. "You're making a mistake. I came here to stop you."

"But I don't have a choice! How am I going to find a husband after this?" I said. Diane shook her head.

"Norman forced himself on me a long time ago and we were married shortly after," she said. "I felt like I didn't have a choice either. When Shelly was born, Norman left me to take care of her."

"How many people has he done this to?" I asked.

"I don't know," Diane said. "I certainly don't think I was the first."

She paused.

"Teera, I know you don't think you have a say in the matter, but you do," she said.

"That's not true Bubby," Pappa butted in. "You have *no* say in this matter. You are never to see this man again and that's final. We will not be speaking of it any longer. That bastard had better not let me catch him around you or I swear I'll split his head open!"

Pappa left me in the room with Diane and Shelly, and I told them everything. It was such a relief to talk to someone that understood where I was coming from. I never wanted any of this, but it happened, and I can only thank God for sending them.

Norman didn't know that Diane and Shelly had sought me out, so he was naturally surprised when he showed up to our house and Pappa was waiting for him with a metal post and the rage of a charging bull. I watched from my window as Norman unsuspectingly strolled up to our front door expecting to see me. Pappa answered and immediately started swinging as Norman unleashed a terrified, high-pitched scream and darted away from the house.

Pappa chased Norman a good distance down the road before finally giving up, but he wasn't satisfied with simply scaring away the man that raped his youngest daughter. Father never got the chance to exact his revenge on Norman personally, but he made sure that someone else would. He put the word out to anyone that would listen, and news travels fast in a small town like Wadduwa. My father didn't care how it happened, but he wanted justice for his little girl.

It was days before I finally gathered the courage to go out in public. Eventually I grew sick of being inside, and the idea of going out for some fresh air sounded rather endearing. I wanted to walk stoically around town and perhaps see a few of my friends. So I dressed up in my best attire and set off to the market, apprehensive, yet hopeful that I could start fresh that morning, and put the past behind me.

Everything seemed so alive as I strolled closer to the center of town, taking time to notice the smell of fresh fish and the sound of distant vendors as I let the sunshine warm my shoulders. Still chilled from days spent indoors, I could feel the sun feeding my skin as my lips magically pulled upwards to form a smile, something I hadn't done since I attended Megan's wedding.

I passed by our neighbor, Deborah, and her two daughters. As I do every time I pass Deborah and her children, I smiled and said, "Hello."

Rather than respond, Deborah stared back at me, her mouth agape. She quickly grabbed her children and hurried them away. I stood confused for a moment. As they kept walking, I heard her quietly tell her children to keep away from me because I was "a rotten girl."

I kept walking. I had forgotten that my father told nearly everyone in town about what happened with Norman. I felt the stares of friends and neighbors as I continued on to the market. The busy street market eerily declined in volume as I approached. A priest from our parish passed and paused to stare disapprovingly before shuffling away. Behind him, I noticed a group of my parents' friends from church looking in my direction and whispering among themselves.

Suddenly unwelcome in my own village, I quietly bought my fish, hung my head in shame, and left. I ran home as fast as I could, scuffing my white Sunday shoes that I had so excitedly laced up no less than an hour before. With each quick step towards home, I felt as though I was running in place, like the earth was stopping me from moving. When I finally got through the door to our house, the only thing I could think to do was cry.

I carried on for the next few weeks like a ghost, numb to feeling and avoiding confrontation whenever possible. I stopped seeing my friends from Wadduwa, which was convenient because they did not want me around anyways. I went from being the happiest girl in town to a despicable and notorious slut overnight. Children were no longer safe around me, and at the confusing age of seventeen, I felt as though this reputation would follow me for the rest of my life.

Depression lent itself to exhaustion; I quit my track team, and with no more upcoming races to train for, stopped running altogether. To avoid ridicule, I refused to leave the house, choosing instead the company of a quiet tree in our backyard where I would sit for hours in one of the few places that I could be alone. In the afternoons I would watch leaves fall and count the days since it had happened. I hoped that if my tally got big enough, I just might learn to forget the memories of my tormented adolescence.

III

When the harassment got to be too much for me I moved in with my sister, Margaret, who lived closer to my college. She had the space to let me rest my head for at least a few months, but once I finished school, I had to look for another option. I still didn't want to go back home, which meant the only other option for me was to go back to Amparai to live with Sheila.

Dasa was still in the house. But it didn't seem like he would be for long. The incident with me was not the first, and evidently not the last time that Dasa had hurt my sister. The two of them had separated by the time I started living there. They had not completely divorced. Dasa was still under the illusion that their marriage might be worth saving. He lived in his own apartment, and visited frequently to see his daughter.

Sheila set me up with a job at the company she worked for. It was a desk job performing clerical work for Brown & Company, which manufactured Massey Ferguson Tractors and Triumph Herald Cars. The job paid decent money, and I really enjoyed the work. The people in the office and on the factory floor were all very friendly, and even better, none of them had known me from before.

My co-workers were all very close with each other and they opened their doors right up to me. It didn't take long before I felt like I fit in with the rest of them. Men from the factory would crack jokes with each other. Those of us in the office filled the hours by pushing papers and telling stories.

For the first time in months it felt like I was accepted. It felt so redeeming. I could actually look forward to social interaction when I got to work, and it felt good. Before long, I forgot all about my reputation back home, and I started to feel like myself again.

Every morning I would greet people as they passed by my desk. They would always briefly retort, normally shrugging the words, "Hi Teera" as they made their way to their stations. However, one man in particular made it his daily routine to spend a bit of extra time and stop by my desk.

"Good morning, Mr. Silva," I'd politely offer, as he'd confidently make his way through the door.

"Good morning, Teera," he'd always start with an endearing smile, "how are you today?"

I would always kick myself for never having anything better to say, but each morning I would offer the same answer, "I'm doing very well, Mr. Silva. How are you?"

For several weeks he always responded almost the same way, shrugging his shoulders gently and saying, "Good, for the most part. But now that I'm here, my day is really looking up." Then he'd smile and continue on his way. We followed that same routine for maybe three weeks. My stomach would flutter when he passed by, and in my heart, I was hoping he felt the same.

One Friday afternoon, Sheila mentioned in passing that she would be going to Kalmunai the next day. I didn't really think anything of it, until Silva stopped by my desk later that afternoon. He told me that he would be working overtime on Saturday, and that I should stop by the office to say 'hello'.

The next day, I patiently waited for Sheila to leave, checked to make sure the maid didn't notice, and slowly snuck out the back door. Even after I safely got out of the house, I was still nervous that I would get caught. Scared as I was, I still walked to the office, stepped through the door, and stood by the wall.

"Hello Teera!" his face lit up when he said it. "Give me just a second."

He was shuffling through a big stack of paperwork in front of him. I patiently waited for a few moments. When he had finished, he stood up from his desk and walked confidently toward me. My legs were shaking as he approached me, I didn't know what to do. He embraced me and we hugged. I felt like I was going to melt in his arms. He then turned his head and he kissed me with the kind of intensity that comes from someone who has wanted to do so for too long. We both did.

When we parted, he looked me in the eyes and said, "Girl, I love you."

He kissed me again as I mumbled the words, "I love you too, Chand" into his lips.

We often called each other 'Chand' and 'Girl' ever since then. When we stopped, he smiled and said, "I remember the day you walked into the office with your sister." It was the first time Silva and I had seen each other. "Your sister asked me to teach you how to write a Paragon receipt. You made a mistake and tore the receipt into pieces like a little child."

I was slightly embarrassed that he brought that moment up, but it didn't matter. As long as he kept staring at me with those eyes, he could say whatever he wanted.

He laughed and kept on telling the story. "You had no idea what you were doing in an office! I never even got the chance to tell you that the receipt was important. I had to paste together each piece of that receipt so I could get all the numbers back in order!"

We both laughed, I felt bad that he had to do extra work because of me. "You looked irritated with me when it happened," I said.

"Yes," he admitted. "For a minute I was, but once I got the receipt back together, I couldn't help but laugh. You were so funny, and unique, and carefree. That was the moment I fell in love with you, Teera. It was the moment that I knew I couldn't live without you."

He had both arms rested on the wall over my shoulders. He leaned in to kiss me again, but before he did he stopped and said, "I will never let you go out of my life."

I was giddy, I was happy, I was in love. I felt goose bumps running up and down my arms. My heart rushed as I leaned in to kiss him back. Right as I did, I caught the glint of a familiar automobile casually rounding the corner just outside of the office. It was Sheila. I couldn't imagine that she had gotten back from Kalmunai so soon, but there she was.

I ducked under Silva's arms and ran out the door to get back to Sheila's house before she did. When I returned home, my sister was waiting for me. She started yelling before the door even opened. She had seen me running from the office and demanded to know what I was up to. She figured I was seeing a man, but she hadn't seen enough to know for sure.

I ran past her and went straight to my room. I turned my head so that I could hide the enormous grin on my face. I didn't care that Sheila was angry; I knew she had nothing to worry about. I was in love! And with someone that wasn't going to hurt me, with someone whom I knew would, in the end, take care of me.

The next day Sheila and I calmly talked about it. She didn't know Silva personally, but she knew of him, and he seemed to have a good enough reputation at work. In all reality, she wasn't worried about me seeing this man. She was worried that Silva didn't know about Norman. I hadn't told Silva yet, but I knew I had to. I just wanted to wait for the right time.

Chandra de Silva, or Silva, as we all called him, was about as gorgeous as a person could get. He had an impeccable complexion with soft hair that sat gently above his brow. His eyes were deep and entrancing; I thought I would be lost in them forever. He was polite and compassionate; the absolute embodiment of everything that I could ask for in a man.

We began seeing each other every day, and even though I kept our romance a secret from my sister and her husband, the pieces started coming together and it all just felt right. It was easy keeping this secret from the two of them because I didn't want to spend time at the house anyways. They were beginning to argue relentlessly and it was best for all of us if I kept my distance.

That was the plan at least, until one day when I came home from work to the muffled sounds of the two of them yelling at each other. I braced myself before entering the door. But this time the emotion in the house was different as I immediately noticed the discouraging look on Sheila's face; she was sullen, defeated, and you could tell she had reached a breaking point. I don't know what Dasa had done, but apparently this was the last straw. The two of them went silent as the door creaked open and I awkwardly entered the house.

"Teera," he commanded as I closed the door behind me.

"Yes," I cautiously responded wondering what today's argument could have to do with me.

"You won't be seeing me here anymore."

"Not even to help Sheila with your baby?" I asked, concerned for the well being of my niece.

"No Bubby," Sheila butted in, "my *ex*-husband will be leaving. And that's the end of it. That's final. Right Dasa?" She stared daggers at him from across the room. He kept his composure, looking for some way to appease my sister while he still had the chance.

Sheila left the room to prevent any further discussion of the matter. There was a beat, and Dasa turned to me as if he was looking for answers.

"You finally got what you wanted. Didn't you, Teera?" he said.

"I don't know what you're talking about," the accusation honestly confused me.

"You wanted me gone, and now I'm gone. You and Sheila have been planning this all along. I knew it. I knew it as soon as she brought you to live with her," he said.

"She brought me to help with the baby!" I said.

"She brought you to help get rid of me!" he said.

I didn't know what else to say. His anger seemed so misplaced. I couldn't understand what role I would have played in the two of them separating.

"You're not getting away with this," he went on. "I'm going to make you hurt too," he smiled when he said it.

"How?" I challenged him. He wouldn't dare touch me again.

"Well, how about I go down to Brown and Company tomorrow and tell your perfect little boyfriend about how much of a whore you were back in Wadduwa? What do you think about that?" he said.

"You wouldn't!" I started to tear up. I had no idea he knew about us.

"It would be a lot of fun wouldn't it? Of course, the two of you would probably stop seeing each other. I mean, who wants to marry a whore anyways?"

"I don't believe you," I said. "And even if you did, Silva loves me! He knows me better than that. He would never leave me."

"Oh yeah?" Dasa said. "Just you watch."

The baby was screaming when Dasa slammed the door behind him. I ran into the nursery to hug Sheila. I prayed that Dasa wouldn't be able to find Silva before I saw him the next day. I always wanted to tell Silva about Norman but I could never muster the courage. I couldn't let him find out like this. He'd never understand.

I didn't sleep that night and it showed on my face the next day. I jumped out of bed when my alarm went off, skipped my shower and jogged to the office. For all I knew, Dasa could have been waiting for Silva at the gates to Brown and Company. I figured that if I got there early enough I could stop Dasa from getting to him.

I got worried when my shift started and neither of them had shown up. Reluctant to leave my post in the parking lot, I eventually meandered inside and took a seat at my desk. One long hour later, Silva showed up late to work. He sauntered into the office, his eyes low. He passed by my desk and offered a heavyhearted hello before taking a seat at his own.

I didn't know what exactly Dasa had told Silva, but it hurt to see him react the way he did. I sat at my desk, struggling for something, anything to say so that he could think to smile at me again. Drawing a blank, I devoted the rest of the day to shuffling papers and avoiding eye contact with anyone, particularly the man that I thought loved me.

By the time the day ended, I had given up hope. I trudged to Sheila's expecting to be greeted by an empty home and gentle silence. But my stomach fluttered when I reached Sheila's house to find Silva waiting for me outside the front door. He slowly approached me with a loving smile and said, "Dasa came to see me last night."

"What did he tell you?"

"Why didn't you tell me?"

"What did he tell you?" I repeated my question.

Silva locked eyes with me, "Teera, I don't care about what he told me."

"I want to know what he told you!" I couldn't let it go.

"It doesn't matter, Teera!" Silva stopped me. "I love you!"

"Oh Silva, I love you too! I swear! I never wanted any of this. I want to explain everything."

"I'd much rather hear the story from you than from Dasa," he said.

"I didn't tell you because I was afraid that you wouldn't understand. That you wouldn't want to see me again." I said.

"You were afraid I'd leave you?" he grabbed both my hands. "Teera, I want to marry you!"

Although he was raised as a Buddhist, Chandra conceded to having our wedding in a Catholic church. It was a big step for Silva, and something that his family questioned him about extensively. Silva knew how much my faith meant to me, and I was so gracious that he was willing to make such a compromise.

Shortly after the two of us were engaged, we went to our local church in Amparai to make arrangements. We didn't get very far with our plans because the pastor, Father Peter, refused to allow us to marry in his church. Dasa had found him before Silva and I had a chance to meet with him. He wouldn't listen my side of the story and even though we pleaded, Father Peter refused to give us his blessing, claiming that because of my history, our marriage would be unsanctified. With a Catholic church clearly out of the question for our wedding, we decided to be married at City Hall instead.

Chandra was originally from a remote village called Dodanduwa. He was one of two children. Even though his mother had given birth to thirteen children, eleven of them had died from complications early on. Silva and his sister were the only two children that had survived into adulthood. The son of a fisherman, Chandra came from substantially less than I did.

He was constantly sending money to his mother and his sister back home. So even though he had a good job, he was still on a tight budget. As such, Chandra was a little rough around the edges when we first were married. I did the best I could to help him out with the essentials he was missing.

I bought him new clothes. I still remember how handsome he looked in his new shirt and shoes. He was completely irresistible, and I would have done anything to make him happy. In return he rewarded me by being the most gentle and hard working husband I could have ever asked for.

We managed to find ourselves a crummy little house with a bedroom and a kitchen. It was all we needed. The two of us were happy enough just being together. Some workers from the Massey Ferguson workshop volunteered to help renovate the place, which meant they practically moved in every weekend for about two months.

Some days we had three workers in the house, other days it was as many as eight. They were filthy, they used terrible language, and Chandra and I absolutely adored having them around. They would spend the day talking trash between each other, occasionally rousing us in the mix. Chandra would help and I would contentedly watch from the kitchen, preparing lunch. That's all the workers ever asked for: beer and lunch. They knew we couldn't afford their labor; they just wanted to help us.

I still wasn't used to the saris that Sheila had given me but I was happy to wear them anyways. That sari meant

I had actually become a woman. After so much doubt, life was finally turning out just like I hoped it would, and every morning Chandra and I would awake next to each other with loving grins on both our faces.

Regardless of Chandra's initial concerns, I was well received by his family when I first met them. Chandra's father, Elias, had three brothers and one by one they began to take a liking to our relationship. Between the three of them, we had so many invitations for dinner every time we visited Dodanduwa that it was hard to keep up. We started making our visits more frequent and after some time, our presence began to wear on Chandra's mother, Leela, and his sister, Sirimathi.

Leela and Sirimathi had a history of jealous antics. I wasn't the only person who was suspicious of them. Silva's closest cousin, Kumara, warned me about them, and encouraged me not to trust them. They were always afraid of a woman taking Chandra away from them. They really took offense to me when they found out that our relationship was going to stick.

They didn't like that I was a Catholic, they didn't like how I dressed. They thought I was overly sophisticated because I came from a bigger town. Most of all, they could tell that Chandra really loved me. I never wanted them to dislike me. I never disliked either of them. I just wanted to have a good relationship with my in-laws.

Chandra's father, on the other hand, could not have been happier that the two of us were together. He could see that we were both happy and he did what he could to nurture our relationship. He often visited Chandra and me in Amparai. Every time he came, he would regale us with stories of how Leela and Sirimathi tried to convince him not to come. I think he took some pleasure in stirring them up, but he also was not about to change his mind. He always said that the two of them were just being dramatic.

Leela and Sirimathi lived with Elias in a humble, yet impressive, brick home on several acres of land by the beach in Dodanduwa. Elias and his brothers owned the property, which was bequeathed to them from their father. It was the understanding between the brothers that the eldest nephew out of all of them would eventually take ownership of the house and the land when he was married.

The eldest nephew was Chandra's cousin, who took vows to become a Buddhist monk when he came of age. His vows forbid him to take a wife or own property. Therefore all eyes were on Chandra as he was the next eldest in his generation. We were flattered by the thought of eventually owning the property, but to us it was an afterthought. We didn't really feel like we needed it.

Truth be told, I was hoping that Elias would have a change of heart and just hand the property down to Sirimathi. It was a long shot, but it seemed like it would have been the easiest option for him. We were happy enough as it was in Amparai and we did not want to relocate. Besides, I didn't want to live in the same town as my in laws. That would have just been too awkward. I felt strange enough around them as it was.

Back at home; on a calm and sunny evening I casually lugged my heavy stomach home from work. I was halfway through a fish curry for dinner when the muscles in my abdomen contracted violently. The pain was so intense that I dropped my boiling pot, making a colorful mess of smelly fish meat and bright curry all over the kitchen. I gripped the counter, attempting to keep my balance.

I called out to my sister who was close by, "Sheila!" I screamed. "It's happening! What do I do? What do I do?"

"Calm down!" She said, "Try to breathe, we'll get you to the hospital, Chandra can meet you there."

It was hard waiting a few more seconds but soon enough the outline of my first son, Jude, became clear in the blinding rays of the OR spotlight. The doctors had to stop me from trying to hold him so that they could have a chance to cut the umbilical cord.

It was in that moment that my life truly felt complete for the first time. I felt a sense of purpose that I previously thought impossible. It was a sense of fulfillment that to this day I find absolutely inexplicable. Chandra stayed with me the entire night in the hospital, and the next morning we went home to begin our lives as a family. The following months flew by in a torrent of ruptured sleep and frantic attempts to attend to our new baby boy.

The same day Jude took his first step, I went into labor with my second child, a daughter named Shirlene. I chose to give birth to Shirlene at home and Mamma came to assist with all the arrangements. The midwife wrapped my beautiful baby girl in a blanket and handed her to her proud father. He smiled nervously at the baby and then at me, and I smiled back, consoling. I could see the relief in mamma's eyes. I just remember thinking the whole time that I was living my childhood dream.

Within two years of marriage we had a son and a daughter. Our home quickly became a noisy ruckus of fun, games, and meals for four. The house became especially crowded during the weeks when Mamma and Pappa would stay to help take care of their new grandchildren.

The house had no electricity or running water, but we got by as we could. Water would normally come by way of a bowser truck that would drop off two barrels to the house every week. Money was always something to consider, but Silva and I never fought about anything like that. We had what we needed, and that's all we cared about.

We could not have been happier in that dinky little home with our two beautiful children. Jude and Shirlene quickly became the talk of the town. Everyone used to say they looked perfect, like little dolls. I had never been so content and the weeks began flying by as I watched my children grow in our happy home.

There was a day when Chandra's father came to us looking for money to help save his fishing business.

We didn't have much, if anything, to give him. He and Chandra were talking about it one day; I overheard the conversation from the next room and offered to pawn my jewelry to raise money. Chandra and Elias didn't like the idea; they both didn't want me to have to do that. But I wanted to, and I wouldn't let them take no for an answer.

I kept the pieces that meant something to me. Of course my wedding ring wasn't going anywhere. And I couldn't let go of these gold bangles that my mother had given me when I was a girl. But the rest of it was just stuff. There were necklaces, bracelets, and earrings. Some of them even fetched a pretty good price.

Helping my husband's family was important to me, and it felt so good to be able to give something back to them. Elias was so happy when he was able to meet his expenses and keep his boats out on the water. Chandra made sure that I knew how thankful he was, but to me it didn't matter. I was just happy that I could do something like that for the man that I loved and adored.

It was a curious occasion when Silva and I received word that Sirimathi was going to be married. She insisted I be her wedding planner and I was curious as to why. I figured maybe her disdain for me had subsided when she was finally engaged. Maybe this was her way of letting bygones be bygones.

The ceremony was to happen quickly, so I didn't have much lead-time. In a few exhausting days Sirimathi and I pulled together an impressive ceremony. We even had enough time to arrange for a stunning sari for her to wear. The two of us began to feel more comfortable around each other as we worked together to make this wedding perfect.

Typical of a Buddhist wedding, the Poruwa ceremony took place at the bride's house. By the time all the guests had shown up, Sirimathi and Leela's peaceful home was a madhouse of celebration. Boisterous characters from the groom's side invaded the house with a barrage of flowers, incense, and beer.

Sirimathi was to marry a man named Somapala, who was one of Leela's distant relatives. Somapala's family proposed the marriage. Sirimathi and her parents were impressed by Somapala's promising position at the Department of Agriculture in Polonnaruwa. He lived in a home provided by the government, which also made him particularly appealing. Government homes were more comfortable to live in compared to most of the other homes you would find in Sri Lanka. They were spacious and well insulated; a cozy place to raise a family.

Chandra's uncles, on the other hand, were especially unimpressed by Somapala's upbringing. Somapala's family had an ill reputation in Dodanduwa. They were known thieves with a violent past. Somapala's brother Gunapala was skilled with a knife and available for hire. He'd killed before, and Chandra's uncles knew it.

Sometime during the celebration, I snuck away from the party to get some fresh air. Quietly, I stepped towards the beach behind the house, leaned against some over-turned fishing boats, and gazed out towards the ocean. It was there that I was approached by two of Somapala's uncles. They stared down at me with menacing eyes ruffled below two massive foreheads. They took no time to introduce themselves.

"Well look who it is," said the one on the right.

"Who, me?" There was no one else around, but I was still thrown off by the question.

"I bet you're pretty excited about that house aren't you?" said the one on the left.

"Not really, Chandra and I aren't moving there, we want to stay in Amparai." The two stared at me as if I was putting them on.

"They haven't told you yet, have they?" the one on the right got curious.

"Told me what?"

"The only reason we let Somapala marry Sirimathi is because we thought the house was in the dowry," the one on the left said. "The house, the property, Leela practically promised it to Somapala! She wanted to make sure Sirimathi got the property before you did."

"So are you saying that I am trying to steal the house from Leela?"

"Don't play dumb," the one on the right shut me up. "We looked at the dowry. The property isn't part of it. If the house isn't going to Somapala and Sirimathi, who then would Elias pass it on to?"

"I'm telling you, we don't want the property."

"That's what we thought you'd say," the one on the left grinned through a bushy mustache.

"From what Leela tells me," the one on the right said. "Elias has taken quite a liking to you. Chandra hardly comes back to Dodanduwa anymore and no one seems to mind. You already took Leela's child, now you're taking her house? That's pretty bold, Teera."

"This is ridiculous! How can you even say that? I don't even want the house!"

"That's not how it seems to us. Go ahead and take your inheritance like you wanted, we'll see who has the last laugh." The one on the right said. The two of them cackled, turned, and went on their way back to the party.

The next morning I awoke to a messy house filled with early morning sunshine belching upon the remnants of the previous night's festivities. I went about cleaning up after the party, eager to finish up my duties as wedding planner so I could return to Amparai. Chandra and I had a particularly busy week at work and had planned only a brief trip for the wedding. I was just getting started when Elias and Chandra interrupted me by excitedly entering the room.

"Teera, I want you to sit down," Chandra's father instructed. I took a seat next to the children. "The brothers have decided, and we want you and Chandra to have the house." He and Chandra both eagerly awaited my reaction.

"That's wonderful!" I said, trying to hide the sick feeling in my stomach. Chandra could see the concern in my eye.

"Teera, is something wrong?" he asked.

I didn't want to bring it up in front of Elias because I didn't want to offend him. But seeing this as my chance to say how I really felt, I took a deep breath and spoke up.

"Chandra," I said, "I don't know if we can accept this house. Somapala's family expected it for their dowry. When they found out at the wedding that they wouldn't be getting the house, they came after *me* looking for answers."

"Teera, I don't want you to think about them," Chandra said. "We're just going to own the house, we're not going to live there. Not now at least. We have a life in Amparai. But if we ever want to come back to Dodanduwa, the property will be waiting for us."

"But these men really frightened me, Chandra, I don't have a good feeling about it," I said.

Elias interrupted. "Now Teera," he said. This house belongs to my brothers and me. Not to Somapala's family, and not to anyone else. What we do with this house does not concern them."

"But what about Leela and Sirimathi? Surely they have a say in the matter." I still wasn't sure about the decision.

"They do not have a say in this matter, either. The brothers and I want you to have it," Elias said. "You and Chandra had our first grandchild, the first of our generation. My brothers and I are very proud and pleased with you two. They want to see Jude carry on the family name."

I couldn't argue with that. "I suppose it's best for the family," I conceded.

"Then it's settled," Elias said with a smile from ear to ear. "The house is yours! You'll go back to Amparai. Leela and I will continue to live here. And when you feel the time is right, you may do with it what you wish."

Chandra and Elias embraced to celebrate the decision. I took a moment to let go of my apprehension and appreciate the incredible gift that had been given to us. It meant so much to me that Chandra's uncles would trust us with something as valuable as the family property. Elias and his brothers were proud of us, and the gesture was truly touching.

"Thank you," I said after a pause. "It really means a lot to us."

Later that day, Chandra and his father carved a sign bearing Jude's middle name, 'Chitral', and proudly hung it on the front of the house. For Chandra and his father, the beach house was a reminder of the promise held by the next generation that had just come about. In my eyes it was a dangerous omen for Chandra and me. But Chandra was so proud to have this home named after his eldest son, I couldn't help but be happy for him.

Later that day, the two of us said our goodbyes and began the bouncing journey on trains and busses back to Amparai. Even though we were returning to the safety of our own home, I remained unsettled about the feelings

I had leaving Dodanduwa. Concerned and slightly angry with my husband, I further attempted to convince him that we should never have accepted the house.

"Chandra, I still don't want that house," I said sometime during the ride.

"But why, Teera?" he asked, perplexed. "Who do we have to be afraid of?"

"Those men at the wedding!" I said, "Chandra, they really frightened me. I don't know what they could do to us!"

"Teera, we're safe in Amparai," Silva said. "We're far away from all of them. Besides, we have to honor my father and his brother's wishes."

"Chandra, we can still give it back. Please, I don't want to have this on my conscience."

"Teera, you're being unreasonable," Chandra said. "I see how Somapala and his family may have thought they were getting the house, but they didn't. And there's nothing they can do about it. I know his family doesn't have the best reputation, but that doesn't give you the right to say these things."

"But I…" Silva wasn't hearing any of it.

"You can't just assume these people will hurt you," he went on. "You don't even know them. If my mother and my sister are upset, they can take it up with my father. No one is going to come after us. It wouldn't do them any good."

"Maybe he's right," I thought. However I still didn't feel comfortable with the situation. For the time being, I figured I would keep the peace and hold my tongue, but I would be on my guard. Chandra's word, this time, was not enough to let me feel safe.

There were a few sleepless nights after that long bus ride back from Dodanduwa, but it wasn't long until I got back to life as usual. I was so busy with work and the kids that I learned to forget everything else. By that point, the drama with Chandra's family seemed like a troubling distraction.

My days would normally consist of taking care of the two children along with our live-in errand boy named Kusum. Kusum was incredibly helpful and devoted to his work. He loved to play with the children and never missed a beat when there was a task to be done around the house.

We also had a maid that lived with us named Sanduni. Sanduni was a relative of Somapala's, who was introduced to us shortly after Sirimathi's wedding. Somapala was adamant that Sanduni be our live in maid, claiming that we needed the help and she needed the work. We were happy to take her on, and she brought her daughter, Sandamali with her. Before long, Chandra and I began to appreciate the extra hand. She was scant about the details of her personal life, even though she became very close to our family.

Sanduni was in her forties, and a single mother. At her age, in her caste, it was not likely that she would find herself in another marriage. Any romantic interests she had would only be flings, and even those would be considered

scandalous by Sri Lankan standards. After a while, there
was talk of Silva and me adopting Sandamali.

Along with Sanduni and Kusum, we were also housing
one of our favorite co-workers from Brown and Company,
a bumbling, lighthearted drunk, named Nissanka. Down
on his luck and unable to pay for his own home, Nissanka
would spend his nights in a donkey bed on the veranda,
exchanging his help for a place to stay.

Honest and endearing, Nissanka had a soft spot in his
heart for Jude and Shirlene. Every day he would stop by
to check on the kids on his way to the post office to collect company mail. After work he'd rush home to play
with the children. He would then dive into a bottle, and
go about cheerfully helping out with whatever household
tasks he could manage.

Kusum, Sanduni, Sandamali and Nissanka were all
part of the family. We relied on them, and they relied on
us. We loved having them around, and I don't know how
we could have kept our household together without them.

Sirimathi and Somapala had talked about coming out
to visit us in Amparai since the day they got married. For
the most part, it was always an empty promise. But when
Somapala lost his job at the Department of Agriculture
for embezzling money, he and his bride were suddenly
out of a house. Somapala assured us that he was framed.

The whole thing seemed off to me. Amparai was hours
out of the way from Polonnaruwa. Somapala and Sirimathi
were short on money, and had the intention of going back

to Leela and Elias' house to stay and get back on their feet. They were distant and short when they arrived. The visit felt strange. None of it made sense to me.

What made less sense was when Somapala awoke the next morning, and announced that he would be headed to Dodanduwa to sell his motorcycle at his parents' house. Sirimathi decided to stay with us.

I walked Somapala to the bus stop that morning. He seemed skittish and distracted, so I kept up the conversation the best that I could. He complained that Leela had not taken a liking to him either, and that he was nervous about moving in with his mother in law.

At least the two of us had that in common. I told him to just ignore her and to not let her get to him. For the first time since I had met him, I felt like I could relate to Somapala. Before we made it to the bus stop, he asked me for 15 rupees for bus fare. I gave him 25 and sent him on his way.

Chandra was worried when I met him at the door that evening. "Kusum left," he said. "He's going back to his village, he's not coming back."

"What? Why? I thought Kusum loved it here," I said. We were both confused.

"He wouldn't tell me at first but when I walked him to the bus stop this morning, he said that a man came into the house last night."

"Last night? When?" Now I was worried.

"He said it happened late last night. He didn't know what the man wanted, he just heard the noise and hid in the other room. This morning he was scared stiff. He didn't even want to eat breakfast, he just wanted to go home," Chandra said. "He told me to be careful and to check the broken mesh near the back door."

"Was anything stolen?" I asked while marching to the backdoor, looking for clues.

"Nothing was stolen, but Kusum said that he saw the man looking in our bedroom window before he came in. He put his hand through the broken mesh to open the door."

I stood by the backdoor and peered over to see Sanduni's room conveniently located right next to the door with the broken mesh. "Chandra," my voice took on a much warmer tone as I asked, "Does Sanduni have any boyfriends you might know about?" I said as if I cracked the case.

"No," Chandra said. "What do you mean?"

"I think you know exactly what I mean," I said.

"You don't think she's sneaking a boyfriend in at night, do you?" Chandra suddenly dawned a fresh smirk.

"Well," I said, "if she hasn't told us, she obviously wants to keep it a secret. Let's not bring it up with her tonight; we'll leave her be. If she feels like telling us, she can tell us."

Chandra smiled and said, "that's fine with me, but the two of them better not keep us up at night!"

"Oh Chandra! Hush up!" He was always kidding with me like that. Satisfied with our story, the two of us went back into the kitchen to make dinner and settle in for the night. We figured that Kusum would come around once he realized that he had nothing to be afraid of.

That evening Nissanka had taken a long time to get home from work. It was dark when he finally showed. Chandra and I were out front on the porch, sharing a beer. He stumbled up to the house, reeking of liquor. His hands were empty, so clearly he had forgotten the bag of rice he was supposed to buy on his way home.

"Teera, I…am…sorry," he managed to slur through numbed cheeks. "You see, I was on the way to the store. That's right, I was on my way to the store from work. That's right. And I met a new friend! He got us drinks… boy did we get some drinks."

Chandra and I both laughed at how drunk he was. "Did you at least manage to get the rice?" I asked.

Nissanka looked at his feet remorsefully, thought for a second and realized, "Oh yeah! Well, you see, I forgot the rice. I don't know how… I just… forgot, I guess. Boy Teera, I am sorry. That man at the bar must have poured something powerful in my cup."

It must have been some strong drink, because Nissanka was far more inebriated than we were used to seeing him. Never once had he let his drinking get in the way of his chores, he had the tolerance of a sailor. We didn't mind though; there was plenty of food in the house.

"It's ok Nissanka," I said, giggling to myself. "Go on inside, we'll be in soon."

Chandra and I sat back and continued to stare at the stars as our conversation drifted into a discussion of philosophy. Silva was a man of very few words and I treasured the moments when I could actually get him talking. He was very careful not to speak too much, and would save his breath only for when his words were truly needed.

That night he sat there half drunk on our porch explaining to me the powers of positive and negative energy that our words possess. He believed our speech echoed through the universe directly affecting the karmic forces that dictate our lives. We could hear Sirimathi and Sanduni in the house behind us. The children were asleep, Sirimathi had given them their milk for the night and the two were safely tucked in.

I tried to keep up with the conversation, but I kept feeling like my head was spinning. "Chandra," I said, my eyes wavering. "I'm fascinated, I really am, but I feel dizzy."

Chandra looked around and noticed the feeling himself, "Wow, he said, me too. I'm having trouble moving from my chair," Chandra said as he let his head fall back. He stared at the stars as I began to get up from my seat.

"I think it's best I go lie down for a little while," I said and wandered back into the house.

"I'll be right in behind you," Chandra's words drifted from behind my shoulder.

Drowsier than I typically get from my evening beer, I plopped my body right in the middle of the mattress, instead of on the side like I normally do. My head kept spinning. Shirlene was asleep in a crib next to the headboard. Jude was asleep on our bed, between me and the wall. Silva entered the room and lied down with us, but sleep gripped my eyes before I had a chance hear the familiar sound of his body next to mine.

I must have been knocked unconscious when it happened. My eyes opened to the sound of Silva flailing next to me. As he struggled, a car screeched out from in front of our house. The noise woke up every person within earshot. I rolled over to see what was the matter with Chandra.

He fell to the cement floor and landed face down, causing a loud slapping sound that split through the darkness. I ran out of my room and into the living room. Nissanka kicked open the front door to see what had happened. His eyes met my face and his jaw dropped. He spun around and went running for help.

I turned from the front door. Sirimathi and Sanduni had just run into the living room from where they were sleeping. They both screamed when they saw me. My face was now searing, my head ached and throbbed, and I couldn't form words. I tried to scream but all I could manage was a garbled wail from the back of my throat.

I stumbled back into the bedroom to see to Silva. He was face down and motionless on the floor. I knelt down to roll him over. When I leaned over, I noticed the blood trickling down my forehead. I saw the stains of blood on my shoulder and felt the loose skin hanging from my lip. I felt woozy, and I slumped forward. The back of my neck tingled and my arms felt heavy.

I must have fainted again because it seemed like Nissanka returned instantly. He came running back into the house with Cramer, from work, who lived nearby. I was lying over Silva's body when they found me. The two of them each took an arm, scooped me up, and carried me to a van that was waiting outside. We headed for the closest hospital, which was only a few minutes away.

Spatters of blood stained the seats while Cramer rushed to start the car. I wanted to know where Chandra was, but no one could understand me. My vision spun in a haze and I slipped into unconsciousness again as the van rolled away.

My eyes opened to a hazy red delirium. The three of us limped into the waiting room of the ER. The nurse on duty didn't notice us as my two friends guided me to the desk. His head down, he asked for my name and age, and turned around to grab a clipboard and an in-patient form.

"For God's sake! Just help her!" Cramer commanded. "She's gonna die if she doesn't see a doctor right now!"

The nurse looked up, dropped his clipboard, and ran back to find a doctor. Almost instantly a gurney appeared through swinging doors and three men in scrubs rushed me back to the operating room.

White ceiling and fluorescent lights moved above me as I strained my ears to catch glimpses of what the doctors were saying. I still didn't know how bad my wounds were.

"We'll have to use staples to close up the lacerations on her crown," I understood one of the doctors say. I began to panic.

"The cut did not penetrate the lip line, but I'm not sure if we can save the tongue. It's hanging by an eighth of an inch and we'll have to re-attach it," another doctor said as I writhed in terror.

"There is no way we can anesthetize this woman," at third added. She's lost too much blood and we don't have time for a transfusion. We have to proceed with the sutures before we lose her."

I struggled to ask what was wrong with me, and as soon as the doctors realized I was conscious, they went silent. The doctor at the foot of my bed commanded, "Teera, I want you to close your eyes and take a deep breath."

There was a quick beat before I felt the sharp sting of a needle digging into my flesh. The first doctor took a long, black, string and began threading my lip while the other shaved my hair to clear the area around my head wounds. I flexed my muscles as best as I could to prepare myself for the initial sting of each stitch. I got through about four of them before my vision went blurry and then, dark.

When I awoke, Margaret was waiting for me in a chair across from my bedside. The light was blinding before my pupils had a chance to adjust. Margaret's figure slowly became clearer, her eyes filled with excitement, "Bubby! Thank God!" she burst out crying.

My vision shifted to see the pink and white dress that I was wearing that night, crumpled up in the corner and soaked in blood. I struggled to mumble a few words. I wanted to know what happened to me, but stitches gripped the muscles in my cheeks and mouth, making movement impossible. I tried to talk from the back of my throat, but my tongue was numb and stitched right through the center.

"Don't try to talk!" Margaret stopped me, "just rest. You've been unconscious for almost an entire day now. You and Chandra were both hit with a knife. We think it was a machete. We still don't know who did it." Her eyes went grim as she tried to skate around the details of what she learned while I was comatose.

"Your story was in the newspaper this morning, everyone is talking about it. Your friends have been lining up to visit you," she said. "As soon as Mom, Dad, and I found out, we all jumped in the car and came here as fast as we could. The others are on the way."

"What about..." I struggled to begin the sentence.

"Don't worry about Jude and Shirlene," Margaret instinctively finished the sentence for me. "They're safe with us, they didn't even wake up the night it happened. They were asleep until almost ten o clock the next day.

Margaret gave me a minute to process the information. Her expression changed slightly as she went on, "they took Chandra to a hospital in Batticaloa so that he could get the treatment he needs," she said. "His wounds are more severe than yours." She attempted to make it sound like Chandra was going to pull through. I wanted so badly to believe her, but I could not shake the images I had of him lying lifeless on the bedroom floor.

Margaret waited for my reaction, but she received little expression from my sutured face. She waited a beat and went on to say, "Bubby, I know you can't speak right now, but there are some policemen that are waiting to ask you a few questions. They've been here, guarding the door since the night it happened."

Police? How was I going to talk to the police? I couldn't even tell the doctors where it hurt or what I had seen because my face was too maimed to move. I still had no idea who had done this. And where did they really take Chandra? Was he OK? Was he still alive? "Dear God," I pleaded, drowsy and feeble, "please let this be a nightmare. I want to go home! I want to wake up! Who are these people in my room? Who did this to me? Why is this happening to me?"

Two policemen entered the room with Somapala following them. What was he doing here? What was Chandra's brother in law doing hanging around the police? I hardly even knew the man and here he was moping into my room and sheepishly settling himself next to my bed. I wanted to say something, but I couldn't. Instead I silently waited for the police to take out their notebooks and get started.

They asked me a few simple questions, "How do you feel?" and so on. I tried to answer, but since my tongue was no use, they kept it to 'yes' and 'no' questions.

"Teera," the first officer asked, "do you know what happened to you?"

I shook my head heavily to indicate "no."

"Teera," did you see who did this to you?" the officer proceeded.

Again I slowly shook my head loosening up the saliva and dried blood on my gums.

"Teera," the officer said, "do you know who *might* have done this to you and your husband? Is there anyone that may have something against the two of you?"

I remembered the men who threatened me at Sirimathi's wedding, but I never thought that either of them would be capable of committing something so heinous. So I went with the best answer I knew at that point. I shook my head heavily to indicate a remorseful "no."

The police, frustrated, put away their notebooks. Somapala had been hanging on to my every word. When the police wrapped up their questioning, he looked a lot less tense.

"OK, officers," he butted in, "I think it's time Teera got some rest. What happened to her has truly been traumatic and she needs time to heal." He led the officers out of the room and disappeared down the hall.

The investigators had not yet left when I remembered the warning that Kusum had given Silva. I remembered the man whom we assumed was Sanduni's lover. Maybe Kusum could recognize him. At the very least it was something to give the authorities.

I made a signal to Margaret who fetched me a piece of paper and a pencil. Carefully, I sat upright and scrawled out a message to her identifying Kusum and explaining his warning to Silva and me. She went out into the hall, told the officers that were on duty, and they took it up with the detective that was assigned to our case.

Kusum didn't give them anything when the police came to question him. I can only assume he was too frightened to. The detective filled me in that evening and I didn't know how to react. He asked me to keep telling the police the facts as I remembered them.

My bedside window was alight when morning broke the following day. Gentle sunbeams warmed my chilly bed sheets and I wiggled my toes when they first felt the heat. My eyes opened and I lay relaxed, flat on my back. My head was clear as I curiously greeted the unfamiliar ceiling above me and pondered the events that led me to this unfamiliar bed. It was a swift, serendipitous second, when I first woke up, where I had actually forgotten that I was hurt.

I tried to sit up and yawn but abruptly stopped when I felt the familiar sensation of fresh sutures in my cheeks. Searing pain came screaming from my skull. Very quickly I was reminded of exactly where I was, and exactly how I got there. The reality of that hospital room came crashing down on me like a terrible nightmare and I tried to hold as still as possible. I couldn't let myself cry. I knew I would break my stitches if I did.

I gained my composure, took deep breaths, and calmed myself. Soon after, the nurse came in with medication and a copy of the newspaper. She flopped bundled pages on the nightstand next to me and I craned my head to make out the headline, "Husband Dead on the Spot; Wife in Critical Condition," it read. My heart sank. Chandra was dead. Margaret couldn't tell me because the doctors were afraid the news would be too much for me to handle.

I couldn't hold back any longer. I choked on the lump in my throat as a few soft tears gathered blood from my cheek and dripped gently on my stale, hospital pillow. The nurse noticed my sudden change in mood while she was adjusting my I.V. She matched my face with the picture on the front page, carefully grabbed the newspaper, and left the room with it. I was glad she did – I already knew everything I needed to know.

More time passed before I had gained enough strength to see my son. My brother, Anthony brought Jude to the hospital for a visit to his mother whom he hadn't seen in days. The door opened as I eagerly looked for my precious little boy, the only thing that could lift my spirits from this bed. The door creaked open as he nervously entered the room, curious and anxious to see me.

But when Jude looked up to see his mother, his eyes widened at the sight of a freakish creature with enormous gashes and a half shaven head. My own son couldn't recognize me and grabbed his uncle to cower in fear. Anthony tried to calm him down, but the two eventually exited the room, leaving me alone with the sound of my son's frightened cries drifting steadily down the hall.

Our families gathered for Chandra's funeral a few days later. I was still in the hospital. Margaret visited me afterwards. She told me the event was pathetic. Pappa broke down at Chandra's feet and wept like a child when he approached the casket. My family took a picture of my husband at the viewing so that they could show me how peaceful his face looked frozen in that coffin. I prayed that his soul be at peace and that his spirit would remain with us.

Margaret mentioned that Somapala's brother, Gunapala, also attended the funeral. She cocked her head to the side as she went about tidying up my room. "I don't feel like he knew Chandra's family very well," she said. "Was he close with Leela and Sirimathi?"

I shrugged my shoulders. I honestly didn't know.

"A bandage was wrapped around his hand, and everyone in the family was curious about it so I asked. He said he cut his hand with a machete while chopping fish."

"Did Leela or Sirimathi say anything?" I gurgled from the back of my throat. After a few days of healing, my mouth had loosened up enough to form short sentences.

"The two of them were hysterical at the funeral. But they kept looking around to make sure people were watching them. They have been acting strange ever since it happened," Margaret replied.

"How else?" I asked.

"They were saying that you were dead when we got to the hospital. They were all torn up about it, said they couldn't believe it. It wasn't too long after that, when the doctor came out and said you were going to make it. We were all so excited, Bubby! But they looked different, they looked…worried. They left pretty soon after that. They didn't even come to see you."

"Why did they think I was dead?"

"I don't know. They just assumed you were," Margaret said. "I talked to Nissanka about it while we were waiting for you to wake up. He said he saw Sirimathi raiding the almyra, looking for jewelry the next morning. There was still blood on the floor!" Her voice got grim, "Bubby, she took the wedding ring off of Silva's finger when the medics took him from the house."

There were still police officers guarding the door to my room when I was finally released from the hospital. I was given a few days to rest before being transferred to a facility in Colombo for head trauma. Marcus took me to his sister-in-law's house before we made the trek to the city.

I was glad to be going home with Marcus to somewhere that wasn't my own home. I was never going to go back to that place. I couldn't. Not with the fresh stench of my husband's murder still rotting in those hallways.

In those days I took time to let my children grow more accustomed to their newly disfigured mother. Each day was another opportunity to mentally prepare myself for my new life with my new face. I had not looked in a single mirror since before the attack. I didn't think to examine my mangled face. It was the least of my worries at the time.

When I finally caught my reflection in the bathroom mirror that day, I was mortified. I could hardly recognize myself. A gigantic gash, still pink and raw, extended from my left cheek, across my upper lip, and down into my right cheek forming a permanent frown. Sutures crawled across my face like heavy, black rope. Several of my teeth were missing, and my eyes were bloodshot red. My cheekbones were hidden below black-and-blue skin that protruded like a swollen jackfruit.

After years of growing it out, my hair, my beautiful, long, dark hair was gone. The majority of it was shaven off during surgery. Replaced instead by dark lines of lacerated skin, stitched shut to stop the bleeding.

I didn't know who was staring back at me. The only thing that was familiar on my body was the long blue dress I was wearing. Now I understood why Jude could not recognize me. I couldn't recognize myself. "Oh my god, I look like a monster!" I thought as I gazed into my red eyes, hanging with sadness. "What have they done to me?"

I tried to reason, telling myself that the swelling will go down. But what about these cuts? Those would leave scars, big, noticeable scars. I was thin and weak, like all the life had been sucked out of me. And it had. Whatever humanity and beauty I had developed throughout the years was violently hacked from me with four crushing blows from a machete.

The first thing to do was wash the dried blood from my skin. I hadn't bathed in nearly two weeks because I couldn't risk re-opening my wounds. Even if I could bathe, I didn't want to. I didn't want to do anything that made me feel good about myself. My hair had matted on top of my head, stuck together with dried blood, dirt, and body oil built up from days of poor hygiene.

Marcus' wife Charlotte helped me straighten out the crusted, knotted hair that hung from my skull, slowly scrubbing and pulling a comb through the patches of my head that were not shaved bare. The process was exhausting as she had to take great care to avoid pulling on my tender skin. By the time she finished, my wounds had taken on a much less gruesome appearance.

They instead looked eerie, as I could now count every stitch as it shone through clean skin. I began tracing over the scars trying to recount the incident. Judging by the location of the scar on my lip, our assailant must have been aiming for my neck, and I can only thank God that he missed. I could see where the machete blade entered my cheek and exited the other side. The entry wound was sliced with the type of precision that comes from years of filleting fish. It was a clean cut, deep and deliberate. Whoever did this to me, was clearly experienced with a knife.

My heart broke as I realized how painful Chandra's death must have been, and hope seemed fleeting as I remembered how alone I was. Yet despite the rush of sadness that overcame me, I had a reason to be thankful I survived: it was my children. My children needed at least one of their parents with them as they grew up. Now that their father had been taken from them, it was up to me to raise Jude and Shirlene by myself.

I shook my beaten body out of bed the day my flight left for Colombo. Before leaving, I looked at myself in the mirror anticipating a day of being out in public, but only quickly glanced. I didn't care about my appearance. I stood like a statue as Mamma wrapped me in the white sari that Chandra had just bought for my birthday.

I was supposed to wear that sari to a party the following week. We were going to celebrate my birthday, but we were also going to celebrate our wedding since there was no reception when we were married at City Hall. The sari had a gold pin, and a friend was going to sew roses into the fabric. Silva was murdered before I had a chance to give the dress to her.

"My poor, broken child," my mother said to Marcus after helping me dress, "there's nothing left of her but skin and bone."

While leaving the house I took a deep breath letting the bright sunlight constrict my pupils, dilated from days of resting inside. Slowly, we made our way to the Amparai airport where a small crowd of friends and co-workers were waiting to wish me well before I set off for Colombo. The feeling was strange as I slowly passed through the eager crowd like a zombie – a walking corpse in a white sari. I was lethargic, weak and dizzy with a stomach churning from painkillers.

I wanted to be happy to see my friends, but instead their presence was a paralyzing reminder of how helpless I had become. Shifting my vision from expression to expression, I absorbed empathetic stares from the haze of familiar faces that engulfed me like a heavy fog. I floated through them slowly and silently, ominously. I felt disconnected from them, disconnected from reality, a third party to the unfolding of my life's greatest misfortune. It felt as though I was attending my own funeral.

I remember seeing my manager from Brown and Company, Arthur. He was smiling and carrying my two children. The way he held them reminded me of how Chandra would carry them into the house everyday after work. Arthur embraced me before I made my way to the terminal and told me to be strong.

Once in Colombo, Sheila guided me to the clinic and dealt with the paperwork as I slowly shifted from waiting room to waiting room. The X-Rays confirmed a crack in my skull, which could not be fixed by a brace or stitches. My skull would have to heal itself over the next few months. I had to keep the wounded area clean, which meant constantly having to shave my hair.

It was a few days of doctors' visits before I gained the strength to return from Colombo to be re-united with my children. This was my first chance to see my husband's grave, and by the time I made it home, I knew I was ready to see it. He was buried in front of his Uncle Balisingho's home in Dodanduwa under a freshly settled mound of dirt with no marking. Leela advised against a headstone insisting that it would scare the neighbors and bring down the value of his house.

I took the kids to his grave as often as I could while we were in Dodanduwa. We sat on the grass beside his remains, trying to grasp the fact that he was gone forever. I kept thinking back to how sad I was that I couldn't attend the funeral. The more people told me about it, the more I began to grasp the enormity of the event. People came out of the woodwork to pay their respects.

But it was not merely the spectacle of Chandra's brutal murder that drew so many people. Chandra truly had a dynamic sense about him. He was incredibly endearing and had countless friends around town. People respected him because he was a humble and caring person. His reputation spread mostly through friends' stories and elaborate fish tales, and everyone in Dodanduwa had something to say about 'Chandra.' When he was murdered, the news put a speech-stopping lump in that entire town's throat.

Things quickly became sour between Chandra's family and me. Sirimathi and Leela had been acting suspicious ever since the murder, but I still had no proof they were involved. Sirimathi nevertheless had the audacity with me to let him keep Shirlene for a few days. I didn't like doing it, but I thought that certainly she would be safe with her own grandfather.

On the way back to Wadduwa, with Jude asleep on my lap, he broke an awkward silence that had fallen over the two of us.

"Teera," he said. "I know that Somapala's family was behind the murder."

My stomach dropped. "How do you know?" I knew he was right, but I wanted to know how he knew.

"I should have never trusted those people. They never wanted Siri as their daughter, they just wanted the house," he went on.

"But how?" I returned him to the point.

"I can't prove it. But I know it. I know it was them. Teera, I'm so sorry."

"But how do you know it was them? And why did they have to kill Chandra?"

"Teera, I don't know," he began to well up. "I don't know why they had to kill my boy."

"I could see why they would want to kill me," I said. "But Chandra?" now *I* was starting to cry.

I didn't want to tell Elias that I thought Leela and Sirimathi had something to do with it. I didn't have the heart to. But I knew they did. To me it was obvious.

That night I again replayed the evening in my head. I remembered that Silva and I slept on opposite sides of the bed that night. We were both so drowsy we just weren't paying attention. I plopped my body in the middle of the

to accuse *me* of being responsible for Chandra's
She claimed I was having an affair with another ma
came to murder us both.

Elias advised that it would be best if I left tow
offered to take the children and me back to my pa
home in Wadduwa. I didn't understand it at the tim
he was trying to tell me that my life was still in dang

That night Elias pulled me aside to address one
item of business before we left the next day.

"Teera," he said, "I know this is not somethin;
want to think about, and personally I don't thin
something you should be thinking about right now.

"Our house in Amparai?" I guessed.

"Yes Teera," he went on. "If the house is not goi
be lived in, I think it's best I sell it."

"Yes!" I said, relieved. "I don't need it anymore. I (
want to live in it anymore."

"I know Teera, and you should not have to," he
"What's important right now is that you get better. I
send you the money we receive when the house is sol

His tone changed slightly as he continued, "now
my son is gone," he stuttered as if he was searching
the right words, "I have to make sure that I protect
daughter." The words sounded more like an apology.
stared down at his feet while he spoke.

I signed the house over to Chandra's father the n
morning. My bags were already packed when he brou
out the deed. Once the papers were signed, he pleac

bed, and when I woke up, he was half dead and on my left side instead of my right side.

If whoever did this was sneaking in through the back and scoping out our house in the days prior to the murder, he would have known what sides of the bed Silva and I slept on. He would have been counting on it.

Maybe they just wanted to kill me. Maybe the killer thought Silva was me, and when he realized he made a mistake, tried to finish the job and failed. That made more sense to me than any plan involving Chandra's murder.

Several days passed before I received word on the house. Chandra's father withheld the money he made from its sale, claiming he needed to use the cash for funeral expenses.

I didn't respond to his letter because I knew it was a lie. Our employer, the president of Brown & Company, took care of the full funeral costs in order to help our family through the loss.

I never believed that Chandra's father wanted to keep the cash for himself, and I still don't. I think Leela and Sirimathi wanted it. Elias was bigger than that. He wouldn't have stooped that low.

I could have pursued the money he owed me, but I rather decided to choose my battles. I had lost so much already. In comparison, this was nothing, just another drop in the bucket. In any case I had bigger problems on my hands. That twisted family still had Shirlene, and showed no intention of giving her back. These people had taken everything from me, and now they were trying to keep my daughter.

I couldn't waste any more time so I immediately rounded up the troops. Mother, Sheila, Marcus, Charlotte, Margaret, her husband, and I came up with a plan and headed back to Dodanduwa. We descended upon the front porch of their wretched house ready to do whatever it took to get Shirlene back. Leela, Somapala and Sirimathi defiantly lined up in front of their door, claiming that I had no right to take my own child.

"But Shirlene is *my* grand child," Leela commanded. "I lost my son, at least let me have my granddaughter."

"But she's *my* daughter!" I said.

"Shirlene is happy here, and we still don't know if you're well enough to take care of your daughter. I wouldn't be a good grandmother if I gave Shirlene back," Leela reasoned, with a sudden calm to her voice. I stared back fuming.

"It really doesn't matter what you think," Marcus butted in. "Shirlene's coming with us, and that's the end of it."

"I won't allow it!" Sirimathi blurted, "how can I trust you with my niece? I'm still not sure *you* didn't kill my brother."

"Lies!" Marcus retorted, "*you* killed Chandra and whoever you hired was too spineless to finish the job and murder Teera!"

Sirimathi and Leela stood dumbfounded as if they had just been found out.

"We're taking Shirlene," Marcus said. "Just you try and stop me."

Marcus pushed the two women aside, marched up the steps and took my daughter by the hand. Shirlene grabbed his neck, excited about the possibility of going home with us. We turned and hurried down the front steps before they could stop us.

"We all know what happened that night!" Marcus yelled back at them before he stepped in the car. "We know you were behind it! And I had better not see you near my sister again! Ever! Or else I'll be coming for *you* with a machete!"

Sirimathi and Somapala stormed back into the house while Leela remained on the front porch mouthing quiet insults. A small crowd of neighbors, some of whom included Chandra's relatives, had gathered to watch the spectacle. They cheered as we hurried to our cars.

Dodanduwa was in my past and I was reunited with my daughter. Nothing was more important than making sure my children were home and happy with me. Now focused on healing myself, I started counting the days until I could at least feel normal again. It was an uphill climb that I knew I could only conquer one day at a time.

Sheila, now recently remarried, offered her and her husband, Tony's home in Colombo to the children and me. They had a little room set up for three of us with a small bed and a dresser. Sheila asked if I wanted dinner and I declined.

The kids were very quiet that night, as if they understood that our lives would never be the same. I fed both of them, and they fell asleep. The bed was too small for three of us, so I put a sheet on the floor next to the bed and laid Jude and Shirlene on it.

It was our first night there. I opened the bag of clothes Margaret picked up from my home in Amparai. As I opened the bag it felt like Chandra was there with me; as if he was standing right behind me with a smile on his face, waiting to give me that loving hug that he always gave me when he knew no one was watching.

I pulled out Chandra's pale blue shirt that Margaret had packed along with the rest of my clothes. That was his favorite shirt. He wore it all the time. I hugged the fabric and brought it close to my face. I could still faintly taste his familiar scent, his sweat, his cologne.

I put his shirt on over my nightgown, and lay down in between the kids. I was staring at the ceiling and was so lost in my lonely, little world, that it took me a moment to realize Shirlene was having an asthma attack. She was gasping and wheezing on the floor next to me, I panicked and took her in my arms. I didn't know what to do, so I started shouting for Sheila.

She and Tony came running to the room. Tony knelt beside her and started massaging her chest. When that didn't work, he took her by the feet and held her upside down. Shirlene was scared. She was tearing up, but she couldn't cry because she couldn't breathe. Her breathing settled to a normal rhythm after Tony had held her by her feet for about ten seconds. He slowly handed her over to me and in a few minutes she fell asleep in my arms.

It dawned on me, when the two of them left the room, that Chandra wasn't coming back. I had no husband to help me with my two children. Their father was gone, and I was alone. There was so much I would have to do for myself now.

I put Shirlene down next to Jude and sat on the opposite side of the room with my back to the wall. I cried for my loss, and I cried for my children. I cried for my face and I cried for my family. It was quiet at first, I didn't want to wake the children. But before long I lost control. I was wailing when Sheila and Tony came back into the room to see what was the matter.

They sat next to me and patiently waited until I was exhausted and couldn't cry any longer. I fell asleep with them beside me, my salty tears still drying on my cheeks. When I woke up, Sheila and Tony had gone back to their room. I was alone again, with my two infants, on the floor of my sister's guest room.

Arthur arranged for me to be transferred to a local branch of the Brown Group, making the transition to a new city much smoother for me. It was comforting to have the familiarity of being able to work the same job with the same company, even though I was in a different town.

I assumed that having a new staff of co-workers around me would equate to a fresh start for me. Perhaps having the company of some new friends would help me move on. The only problem was, the supervisors at the Colombo division of Brown and Company didn't give their employees any information on my back-story before I arrived. When I sat down at my desk on my first day of work, several employees around me fell silent. They stared at my fresh scar and whispered softly amongst themselves as I quietly settled my things.

One by one employees would bombard me with requests to recount my story. I found myself plagued with the sympathy of people who claimed that they 'knew what I was going through.' Each re-telling of the incident was just as painful as the last. By the end of the day I had told the story so many times I was ready to scream.

People feigned understanding, but it was hard for them to relate, and I quickly felt isolated. So much for a first impression. From day one, I was 'that woman with the scar' at the Colombo division of the Brown Group.

There was a girl who sat next to me named Manel. She was the only person in the office that approached me as a friend, and not as an attraction. She never asked for my story, she only asked if I was feeling OK. During those weeks I tried to make it through my entire work day without getting up from my desk; I didn't want anyone to see me, and I didn't want to talk about it. I remember Manel would bring me water and check in on me from time to time. I never had to ask her; she could tell how hard it was for me to even be there.

When the sun went down, I found even more reasons to fret for my life. I held my children on either side of me and slept on my back so they never left my sight. The few times I got a chance to catch decent sleep, my rest was ripped away by horrid dreams of my last night with Chandra. I'd wake with my face throbbing and my mind racing. The children often slept peacefully, but I spent many nights staring at the ceiling, praying for morning to come quickly.

I had no sense of security so long as the lights were off. Sleep became a nightly exercise in re-living the event through my nightmares. I remember lying there with my two children thinking, "that's it, this is all of us." There would be no more warm nights sipping beers on the front porch, no more long walks, no loving husband to wake up to.

I looked thin and I felt empty. The stares from strangers on my daily commute were a constant reminder of how much I truly stood out amongst normal society. Riding the bus made me feel like I was on display, so I began walking to work most days to avoid attention.

At work, I became a drone. It was the only place where I could actually escape and focus on something other than my recovery. There was a sense of purpose that I relished, and at the very least, it was a reason to leave the house everyday. Slowly, I was able to find peace as I focused on my work, rather than my problems.

My home had become a dark place where I had the free time to dwell on how different everything was. Pictures of myself with Chandra, with my old face, were only a reminder of what had been taken from me.

Paranoia plagued me daily, as I knew that Chandra's murderer was still on the loose. I was convinced that whoever did it was on his way to finish the job. My heart would frantically beat to the noises of cracks in the house or the slowing of cars in the street. My constant anxiety showed in everything I did and family would frequently ask why I was so scared all the time. I never had an answer for them.

I often donned inconspicuous clothing and took the children to the park to play with other kids from the neighborhood. Shirlene and Jude looked forward to these days where they could run free, and I could have some time to myself. One such day I met an exceedingly polite man from down the street on our way to the park. He said his name was Maxie and he immediately caught my attention.

We began seeing him almost every day at the park and before long, Maxie became close to us. He would always make up some game for the children to play. He'd then sit by me and the two of us would talk while the kids were busy.

I noticed he was different from other men, and it wasn't just because he could somehow see past my scars. Maxie showed a genuine concern and thoughtfulness that I hadn't encountered in what seemed like forever.

Our conversations began very casually. But after a few weeks, Maxie and I started opening up to each other. It was not long before we came to the subject of what had happened to my face. I told him the story and he stared back with his mouth agape.

"We have to do something!" he said.

"What?" I said. "It's over, we've moved away from there. I just want to know that I am safe with my children here."

"But you're not safe!" Maxie argued. "Whoever did this is still out there. And until they're in jail, Teera, you and your family are not safe."

"But what else can I do?" I said.

"I have someone who can help," Maxie said. "He'll help us find the bastard that did this."

Maxie's contact was a prominent politician with a background in law named J. R. Jayewardene. Mr. Jayewardene would later go on to be elected Prime Minister of Sri Lanka in 1977 and I was impressed that Maxie could enlist the help of someone as powerful as him. With a renewed sense of determination, I sat down with Maxie, J.R., and an officer who took notes, in an air conditioned office at the Criminal Investigation Department in Colombo.

I began talking and J.R. began asking questions. Before we knew it, a short meeting with him turned into an eight-hour bout of painfully recounting nearly everything that had happened since I met Chandra.

He agreed to look into my case, and assured me that based on my description, everything we needed to know was already evident. Sirimathi and Somapala had a motive for wanting the two of us dead. Somapala had a suspicious alibi for the night of the murder as well as a brother who specialized in taking lives.

A detective named Shawn was assigned to investigate. He took the case back to Dodanduwa and when he did, Somapala was the only person that he could find. Somapala was arrested and questioned extensively. When it was all over, he was released, free of any charges. Mr. Jayewardene brought us back to his office at the CID and Shawn explained the results of his investigation.

"Somapala was tight lipped," Shawn said. "We didn't get much out of him."

"What do you mean?" I said. "You didn't get anything out of him?"

"Somapala had a perfect alibi," he said. "The night of the murder, he had spent the night at Chandra's parents' house. He was in Dodanduwa, more than ten hours away from Amparai."

"But that doesn't make any sense! Why would he stay the night with Chandra's parents? Leela and Somapala didn't even get along. *His* parents lived in the same village. Why wouldn't he just go there?" I was angry his involvement could be ruled out so easily.

"He most likely stayed there to ensure that he had witnesses. Both Leela and Elias can attest to the fact that he was in Dodanduwa," Shawn said. "He can even use you as a witness to prove his innocence. You were the one that walked him to the bus stop that morning."

"But I never thought Somapala was the one who did it," I said. "We think it was Somapala's brother, Gunapala. He's been hired to do this before."

"That would make the most sense," Shawn said. "But there is still not enough evidence to prosecute him. All we know is that he has a violent history and that he's skilled with a machete. To me the bandage on his hand at the funeral is proof enough, but there were still no witnesses that night. Sirimathi and Sanduni claim that they never saw anyone leave the house after it happened."

"But I know someone left," I said, "We all heard the car from out front, I can't believe that nobody would have seen him."

"What if Sirimathi and Somapala were the ones that hired Gunapala to go through with it?" Shawn said. "She had a motive, a connection to our suspect, *and* she was seen stealing money and jewelry from your room after the attack had happened. Maybe that's where she got the money to pay him."

"I think the answer is right in front of us, Teera," he went on. "I think it's safe to say that Sirimathi and Somapala both wanted you dead. And I'm sure they both had Leela's blessing."

"What about Chandra?" I said.

"I'm not sure Chandra was supposed to be part of the deal. It could have been a mistake. You said you were sleeping on different sides of the bed that night, correct?"

"That's right," I said.

"That man that you said was sneaking into Sanduni's room the day before," Shawn spoke slower.

"I don't think that Sanduni was in on it," I interrupted him.

"Why do you say that?"

"When I went back to Dodanduwa with my family…"

"While you were all arguing over who should keep Shirlene?" Shawn said.

"Right," I said. "It was all very quick, I couldn't understand her at the time. I was so wrapped up in getting Shirlene back, I couldn't think of anything else. But she came out from the door, walked past Leela and told me to take her daughter too."

"Did you?"

"No," I suddenly felt guilty. "I didn't understand what she was trying to tell me at the time. I didn't know why she was doing it."

"What was she trying to tell you?" Shawn said.

"She was trying tell me that she didn't trust Chandra's family anymore; that she wanted her daughter to get away from them."

"So they've been using Sanduni this whole time? You don't think she was on their side?"

"No, I don't," I said.

"So what if Gunapala was using Sanduni to see where you two slept. What if Gunapala struck Chandra first, thinking that he was you?"

"Do you really think that he could be so careless?"

"He had to do it quick," Shawn said.

"Either it was a mistake, or Somapala's family had a reason to want Chandra dead. Do you think they may have wanted the house for themselves?"

"I know they did, Somapala's uncles made that very clear to me at the wedding," I paused to let my own words sink in. "How do you think the children slept through it?"

"Somebody had to have drugged all of you that night, including the kids. I think we can be certain of that." Shawn said. "Who gave them their milk that night?"

"Sirimathi," I said. My heart broke.

"Teera," Shawn changed his tone. "I'm so sorry this happened to you. And I wish I could bring them to justice. I'm afraid there just isn't enough evidence to put anyone in jail. If we don't have any witnesses, any confessions, or any murder weapon, we just don't have a case."

IV

I must have screamed his name a thousand times in my dreams during the year that followed his murder. The sleeplessness wore heavily on me, and dark bags formed under my eyes.

"It takes time."

I heard the expression over and over again in those wretched months. '*In time*' I will learn to cope. '*In time*' my face will heal and '*in time*' my scars may "not be so noticeable."

I knew that in time the memories of my love, my Chandra, would soon disappear. I tried my hardest to hold on to the idea that his presence may still carry me, and yet, in time, I still felt alone.

Despite how I felt, my life had not stopped moving and my children still needed to be fed. I had to be strong so that I could provide for them. It was a task that presented me with a whole new set of challenges. Now a single mother of two, I braced myself for the task of tending to the household while still making enough money to put food on the table. There was no time left to hang on to my sadness. I had bigger problems on my hands.

It helped that I had this new friend, Maxie, to share my burdens with. His full name was Patrick Laurence Cruz Manatunga, but he always went by Maxie. I remember he listened so well when we were first started seeing each other. I was worried about falling into a situation where I would inevitably give my heart away. But Maxie gave me a sense of security that I needed more than anything at that point in my life.

He had an undeniable sense of humor and perhaps that's what attracted me to him. It felt good to laugh again, and we laughed a lot. The children loved his attention and they loved to see that I was smiling.

Maxie was generous, with a soft spot in his heart for the homeless in our town. He was a charismatic, handsome young man with a dynamic personality and the gift of a tongue trained to speak perfect English. He was just fun to be around. Maxie gave the impression that he was part of the 'high society' in town. He carried a confidence and a sophistication that made it seem as though he had a more privileged background than he actually did.

He said he was an executive at a company called Walker and Sons, even though he didn't seem to spend much time at his office. He said he had the freedom to set his own schedule since he was one of the top executives in the organization.

Despite his position, he was always short on money. According to him, his paychecks always went to his family back home. I knew the man was generous, but to me, that seemed excessive. To Sheila, this new man in my life seemed alarmingly suspicious, and deep down I knew her feelings were not unfounded. The situation was too good to be true.

Our marriage arrived and passed quickly. We married within two months of meeting each other. This time, the ceremony was allowed to take place in a Catholic church. It felt so much less significant the second time around, as if it was something I had to do rather than something I wanted to do. I didn't feel the same butterflies I remembered having when Silva and I made our vows at the courthouse.

Maxie sobbed when he proposed. He said that his mother was a heart patient and that our marriage would make her happy before she passed away. Maxie said that she was bedridden and would not be able to make it to the wedding. The day of the ceremony, I met Maxie's sister Ranjani, and brought up the topic of their mother's health. Ranjani was confused by the question. She said that their mother had been dead for sixteen years.

To me, at the time, this marriage seemed like it was the right thing to do. It was a responsible decision for my children, and the only way I could continue to move forward with so little going for me. I was confident that no other man would want to marry me with my face, my children, and my haunted past. To me, Maxie was my only hope to be married and have a normal family again.

Maxie moved in with the children and me, making things a bit more cramped at Sheila and Tony's house. Sheila pretended like she didn't mind the extra company and tried to help us get on our feet as much as she could. We all squeezed into their house and began to settle down like one big family. For me it was a relieving sense of normalcy and a reassuring sign that my life was beginning to look up.

With the money I was making with Brown and Company, I managed to scrape together a small savings. I had my eyes set on a pre-school for Jude that was run by a group of Catholic nuns. I always admired how clean and proper the convent was. The children there looked happy and healthy, so I knew it would be the best place for him to start school.

When I could finally afford the school fees, I took the day off work to enroll Jude. Maxie wasn't at work that day, so he grabbed Shirlene and came along with me. One of the nuns from the school greeted us at the gate and ushered us through the bustling schoolyard. She led us through the convent halls to the administration office where Maxie apparently ran into somebody he knew.

"Sister Martha!" He ran a few steps ahead calling after a hooded nun down the hall. "How are you? How have you been?"

Sr. Martha stepped back but eventually recognized him. "Maxie!" she said, "what are you doing here?" Maxie had a way of charming people. The sister was hanging on to his every word.

"Well," Maxie said, "I have been thinking about sending my son here for quite some time, and I'm here to finally enroll him."

Sister Martha looked thrilled.

"We just want what's best for the kids," he said. "My wife and I are trying to get on our feet and we want to make sure they're taken care of."

Sister Martha looked over to acknowledge me, noticed the scar, and donned a frown of sympathy. "Ah, I see, Maxie, have the two of you fallen on hard times?" she asked genuinely.

"Ah Sister Martha," Maxie said with a grin. "Not in the least! You see, Teera was injured some time ago. It was a tragic accident, and sadly, she lost her husband in the event as well. I'm with her now because I know she wouldn't have anyone to be with otherwise. I mean who would take care of the children?"

"Maxie, you have always had the biggest heart," Sister Martha indulged him. "May the Lord bless and keep you. Step into the office with me and we'll get him all signed up!" Sister Martha opened the door to the office.

Maxie turned to me quietly and said, "don't worry. I'll take care of this. Give me the money for Jude and I'll enroll him."

I hoped that Maxie knew what he was doing. I waited in the hall with the children as I heard muffled laughter bleed through the door and echo into the cinderblock halls. After a few minutes, Maxie emerged like a hero with a grin from ear to ear.

"Great news, Teera!" he exclaimed, stepping trium- phantly through the doorway.

"Jude is in school? They are letting him attend?" I got excited.

"Not just Jude," he said, "but Shirlene as well! Sister Martha told me that both of them could go to school here for the price of one! We can leave the children to start right now! I already paid her and filled out the paperwork."

I didn't know what to say. We excitedly left the children at the convent for the day's lessons and went on our way. We returned to a quiet home, where I basked in silence. Maxie headed out to get drinks in town and left me to myself. I wished he would have stayed, but I figured that he deserved a good drink that night. I always dreamed I could put my children in a private school, and that day, Maxie made it happen.

I proudly went about my motherly duties that week content that my children had their education accounted for. I knew that good grades and stories from the schoolyard were not far off.

About a week after we enrolled the children at the convent, Sheila received a call from the school. When I returned home from work that day, she was waiting for me in the kitchen.

"Sister Martha from the convent called," Sheila was stern. "She said that they have not received any payment for Jude and Shirlene's school fees."

"What?" I didn't understand. "But I gave Maxie the money and he gave it to Sister Martha! What happened to it?"

"I thought that's how it went too," Sheila said. "So I took it up with Maxie, and he said that the convent had made a mistake. I went down there this afternoon to be sure."

"What happened?"

"Sister Martha said that Maxie didn't pay anything that day. He told them he would come back with the money the day after."

"But how? Where did my money go?"

"When I saw Maxie today, he was in town. He had been drinking," she sounded as if she wasn't surprised. "I think we both know where your money went."

"That bastard!" I said to myself.

"Bubby, I don't know what to…" Sheila began.

"What about the children? Where are they?" I interrupted.

"They're still at the convent," Sheila went on, "the nuns offered to take them in for the rest of the day, so long as we figured out the situation with their tuition.

"Sheila," I said. "It took me months to save up that money. I don't have anything left."

I was hoping there might be some other explanation, but no. Maxie stole money from my children, and from me. I don't know how I could ever forgive him.

"Why can't he help you? I thought Maxie had some big-time job at Walker and Sons," Sheila said.

"He says he sends all his money back to his family in Kandy." I said.

"What about *you* and *your* family?" Sheila said.

"He keeps saying that his dad is going to give us part of the profit when he sells the family business this year." The story sounded flimsy as I said it.

"Sheila," I said, "I don't know what I'm going to do."

"I know," Sheila said. "Don't worry, Bubby. I'll pay for Jude. Shirlene is still too young for school, we'll keep her at home for now."

"Sheila, you can't," I didn't want to entertain the idea. "It's too much."

"Bubby, I care about those children just as much as you do," Sheila said. "I want to do this for you, but I also want to do this for Jude."

"Sheila," I stuttered to find the right words. "Thank you! Thank you so much! I'll pay every cent back to you, I swear!"

"This had better not happen again, Bubby."

"It won't," I said. I was surprised it happened a first time. "How could he do this to us?" My eyes filled with tears.

When I approached Maxie about the money, he acted as if the news was just as big of a shock to him as it was to me.

"What do you mean the money's gone?" his eyes darted left and right. "I gave Sister Martha the money before we left. Where else could it have gone?"

Maxie searched my face with his eyes. He wanted to know how much I knew. He continued to deny until I slowly dropped the subject. He swore to me that he would solve the problem, find the money, and make sure that Sheila was reimbursed. I didn't feel like I could believe him.

It was only a few days later that Maxie ran to me, saying that he had received a letter from his father promising our share from the sale of their family's tea estates. He looked as if he had just won the lottery. All we had to do was return to Maxie's home in Kandy to meet with his family and collect what was promised. The trip would take several days. Sheila used our departure as an opportunity to evict us from her house.

"Bubby," Sheila took me aside before we set off. "I told you that I want you to start getting on your feet, but you're not, and I can't take this anymore. You've spent too long in my home. And I think it's time that you find your own. I don't want you two coming back until you have your own place to live."

"I know," I tried to reason with her; "we've been trying, but Maxie keeps draining my money."

"You are starting to sound just like him," Sheila said. "I'm sick of the excuses from *both* of you. Bubby, I know what happened to you was terrible but you have to get past it. You can't keep living like this and you know it."

I knew she was right, but I wish it were that easy for me.

"Jude and Shirlene can stay with me even after you two get back from Kandy. While they're here, you and Maxie need to go look for a place to live."

Maxie didn't take the news too well. I made sure to tell him after we had left town, that way he couldn't embarrass me in front of my sister.

"What do you mean she's kicking us out? Just like that?" he said. "There must be something I can say. I think I can convince her. She'll let us stay."

"Maxie, I don't want to stay at Sheila's anymore!" I cut him off. "I want us to find our own house! I want to live like a real family. I want to be able to take care of each other. Is that too much to ask?"

He didn't respond. Maybe it was too much for him.

"Maxie, it's our only choice," I said.

"Sheila's just angry," he said. "She'll calm down. Give her a week and she'll come around."

"We can't. Not anymore," I said. "It's more complicated than that."

"How so? She's your sister!" Maxie said.

"There won't be any room at Sheila's if we stay there too long,"

"What do you mean?" Maxie asked.

"Maxie, I'm pregnant," I said. "We have a baby on the way, and I think that means it's time we move out of my sister's house. She doesn't want us there; I don't want us there. Please Maxie, when we get back from Kandy, can we stop all this nonsense and find our own home?"

He looked at me as if I presented him with a challenge that was beyond his capacity. "You're right, Teera," he said. "We'll find a place of our own when we get back from Kandy. My father is going to lend us the money we need to get back on our feet. We'll raise our baby in a good home, I promise."

The trip to Kandy was exhausting. Between train tickets, bus fares, groceries and a few bottles of arrack for his father, Maxie had spent my entire month's salary. "Maxie's father had better have money for us," I thought. "Otherwise we are going to have real problems on our hands."

Maxie never brought up the subject of money with his father because there was never any letter in the first place. The whole trip was an excuse to visit home and drink with his dad. When I asked Maxie about it as we were leaving, he shrugged and said that his father didn't have anything to give us.

I feigned like I wasn't upset, but inside I was boiling. We were broke. We had no home to return to, and every day I noticed that my belly felt a little bit heavier. We began the trek back to Colombo the next day. With no money, we couldn't pay for food. By the time the afternoon came around, I was starting to feel dizzy.

We made it all the way to the bus station in Colombo, when my head started spinning and I found myself grabbing a signpost for balance. Maxie looked at me in panic saying that my face had gone pale. Before I could process what he was saying, my knees gave way below me. Daylight shattered into crushing black. I collapsed under the pressure of my own weight while Maxie stared back at me blankly. He looked like he wanted to help, but didn't know what to do.

When I came to, I slowly sat up and looked around at a concerned crowd of onlookers. They stared with grimaces of pity, rather than of healthy concern. Maxie helped me to my feet and guided me to a bench outside of the bus station. He offered a few flimsy suggestions about where we could spend the night before slumping over and falling asleep next to me.

He had been drinking with his father the night before and all afternoon. Now that he couldn't afford another bottle of arrack, his head was beginning to pound from a painful mid evening hangover. He fell asleep next to me, snoring loud in my ear, without a care in the world. He was useless, which meant I was helpless, alone on a public bench in Colombo. I stared at the sky, digging through every corner of my memory, trying to remember anyone nearby that could possibly help us.

The idea crept into my head just as I began to panic. Relatives of Marcus' wife had a room for rent that was only a few miles from my office. Marcus' wife's niece owned the room. She was a successful film actress named Rita Fernando. And although it was a long shot, the room was our only option for a place to stay that night.

After walking several miles from that bench, we arrived at their house like refugees, hungry and exhausted. To our relief, Rita's family welcomed us with open arms and good old-fashioned Sri Lankan hospitality. Rita was gorgeous and elegant, graceful with every step. We had biscuits and tea before Rita showed us to our room, which was clean yet cramped, and to us, looked like heaven.

We both slept very well that night. Since all my money was gone, I couldn't afford bus fare and had to walk five long miles to get to work the next morning. Before the day was over, I managed to secure myself an advance on my paycheck. The money was enough to pay Rita for the room and keep us off the street for at least a few more days.

Two days later, Maxie said that he had found a place for us to live. He excitedly walked me to the house that he had picked, and we looked in the window but didn't go inside. Maxie didn't have the key for the door. The house looked beautiful, and I hoped that we could afford it.

Maxie told me that we needed money for a deposit so that we could seal the deal and move in. Out of cash and desperate to get our family into this home, I snuck into Sheila's house where she had been keeping my jewelry for me.

I didn't have as many pieces as I did the first time I pawned my jewelry. I didn't think that the money it fetched would be enough, but Maxie said that it was. He left with what I gave him and said that he was going to go make the payment.

He came back to Rita's that night with no keys, and no explanation as to where he'd been or what had happened with the house. "I'll get the keys, and we'll move in tomorrow," he said.

The next night he came home again with no keys and no update. "We'll move in tomorrow," he said. "I didn't get around to it today."

He said the same thing the next day, and the day after that, until I dropped the matter altogether. I realized that I, alone, would have to take on the task of searching for a permanent home for my family.

While I kept myself busy at work, Maxie had plenty of time to lounge around Rita's home and sweet talk her family. In a few short weeks, he managed to charm them so much that they anticipated his daily return to the house. Maxie would claim he was coming back from his office; I could smell the liquor on his breath and knew better.

"I know I can find a better woman than Teera," I heard him say once when he didn't think I was listening. "But I know she'd be alone without me. Sometimes it's hard, I know, but I feel sorry for her. And I feel sorry for the children. I want the three of them to be happy, so that's why I married her."

Rita's family ate up Maxie's story and made him out to be a hero for it. I was his charity case and not his lover. In my heart I knew that I was neither.

Housing both of my children got to be too much for Sheila, so I asked my sister, Mary, to take care of Shirlene for me. Mary was short on cash one evening and sought me out for money to buy milk.

While catching a short cab ride that day, I asked Maxie for the few rupees it would take to feed Shirlene that night.

"I don't have the money, do you?" he said as if it wasn't his problem.

"No Maxie," I said, frustrated. "I don't have any money. I gave you my whole paycheck. What did you do with it?"

His face grimaced as he realized he drank away the money we needed to feed our daughter that night.

"Maxie, I don't know what to do anymore," I said. "I don't know how we are going to raise these children."

He looked down and his eyes filled with remorse as if he somehow understood that he had, in fact, failed as a husband. I could see him swell with rage, but I didn't happen to notice his hand rear back.

Maxie slapped me hard across my cheek. The sound of skin colliding with skin silenced the air in the cab. As I welled up, the driver sat stiff, and Maxie grinned like a menace. It was the first time he had done that to me. But I didn't deserve to be slapped. *He* was the one that deserved to be slapped. I didn't know what to do. I broke down weeping because I couldn't do anything else.

Part of the reason Rita let us stay at her house was because Maxie would show up with weekly loads of groceries for all of us to feast on. He always said he bought them from the store but I knew Maxie, he didn't have that kind of money. Rita and her family, on the other hand, were thrilled.

His days without work led to more drinking. As he drank more, Maxie's demeanor began to change. He had always been manipulative, but now Maxie had taken on an aggressive temper that was ignited at even the smallest of mishaps. As time went on he became much more blatant about his drinking, using the security of Rita's home as a place where he could get away with whatever he wanted.

Rita was in fact singing Maxie's praises when the knock came at the door. She cut her thought short and went to answer. She was met at the threshold by two angry storeowners. Both of them owned separate shops in town, and both of them were still expecting payment from my husband.

Rita tried to defend Maxie's honor. "There must be some sort of mistake," she said. "I know Maxie very well. He would never leave a debt unpaid. Besides, he can afford his own groceries. Why would he need to run up a tab with any of you?"

"That drunk Maxie?" the bigger of the two scoffed through a swollen face and a wiry mustache. "He's a bloody liar! The only reason he's eating anything is because he's been conning us in to loaning him groceries."

"He's been bumming around my store too long," said the other storeowner. "The only thing I see him do all day is wait outside and suck down bottles. Everyone knows him because he doesn't do anything else. I'm sick of giving him handouts; I want what's owed to me!"

"You must have the wrong person, I know Maxie better than that," Rita said.

I, however, did know Maxie better than that. So I had to step in to appease the situation. I gathered up the last of my money and used it to pay the men off. I had nowhere close to the amounts they were demanding but the two of them understood that Maxie was conning me as well. They took what little I could give them and mercifully dropped the matter.

"I still don't believe it," Rita said after the storeowners had left. "Teera, did you know about this."

"I didn't know about this, but there are a lot of things about Maxie that I don't know," I said.

"Apparently there are a lot of things about Maxie that I don't know either," Rita said.

"Is he not the person you thought he was?" I said.

Rita shook her head. "I don't want him in my house anymore. He's a fraud and I don't trust him," she said.

"I understand," I said, "but you will have to tell him yourself. He won't listen if it comes from me."

"Don't you worry," Rita said. "I don't think the family and I will have any trouble taking it up with him."

In the meantime, Rita's brother had left for the Walker and Sons office to pay Maxie a visit. My husband had promised him a job as an executive at the company. The only problem was that Maxie wasn't at the office when Rita's brother showed up. No one in the company knew his name. Maxie had never worked there a day in his life. He had been lying to all of us, all along.

I wasn't surprised. It made way more sense than the bogus story of him sending money back to his family all the time. Beyond angry, I was embarrassed that Maxie had deceived me so easily. I packed our things that evening before he came home and again, began looking for a place where we could rest our heads for the night.

At the convenient distance of a few miles and a quick phone call, I was able to get in touch with my brother, Anthony, who offered his home to us. He found a small annex where I was supposed to hold up with my children for a while, but of course Maxie followed me there too. We didn't last long in the annex, and we would spend the next few years bouncing around between countless back houses and spare bedrooms. We never had a home to call our own.

I started to lose my feelings for Maxie when he first swindled Jude's tuition money from us. From there I had steadily become more emotionally distant from him. I wanted to leave him altogether but I had nowhere to go. Even if I did, Maxie would have followed me there too.

I couldn't go anywhere without him hanging onto me, attempting to assert himself as my keeper. He would glare at other men and scare off my male friends. He would call me out in public for being disloyal, drawing stares from disapproving strangers that were within earshot.

My ignorance of Maxie was a castrating force in his life. It demeaned his ego and his emotions slowly got the best of him. I tried to keep my money from him, but he still found ways to drink. His jealousy made him angry and he hit me more often. He would go on tirades at night, screaming and breaking bottles in his path, saying that I didn't love him anymore, and that I was ruining our marriage.

Maxie used sex as a way to assert his control over me. When I lost the enthusiasm to express myself physically to him, his advances turned into abuse. He lost his inhibition for forcing himself on me, and I had no means of refusing him. Pregnant or not, to him it didn't matter. I was no longer safe at home so long as I was in reach of my husband.

I originally thought work would be the one place where my husband couldn't reach me. But the office phone rang off the hook with Maxie's constant calls. The telephone was on the desk of my supervisor, Mr. John. For every one of Maxie's five or more calls a day, Mr. John would answer, scowl, and pass the receiver on to me.

The fact that Mr. John always answered the phone made Maxie nervous. My husband couldn't accept that I didn't have a phone at my desk. He preferred to imagine his own story. He assumed that Mr. John and I were having an affair. Every time he called I would crouch below my desk and cram the receiver into my ear to muffle the sound of Maxie screaming at me. In hushed tones I'd tell him to leave me alone, but the phone calls never stopped.

Of course Mr. John didn't appreciate Maxie calling me at work, but he had also come to understand how tortured my marriage had become. He encouraged me to move away, and gave me ideas for hiding my money. We would make little arrangements, like letting me leave the office earlier on payday to throw off Maxie's schedule.

The schemes worked and I was slowly able to amass a small savings. Still, it wasn't long before my husband realized that he was short on cash. He had come to expect the money from my paycheck, and when it wasn't there anymore, he panicked. When his lack of cash led him to run out of booze, he looked to me to fund a quick relapse.

I was out back, drawing water from the well when I saw him staring at me from about twenty feet away. He had a sinister grin on his face.

"What happened to your check today, Teera?"

The check wasn't with me. That day I had gone straight from work to Sheila's home and left it with her for safekeeping. He wasn't even supposed to know that Brown and Company was paying my annual cost of living check that week. His eyes were bloodshot and had sunk into the back of his head. His steps were staggered and he laughed as he approached me. His hand reached to his back pocket and Maxie slowly brandished a long fishing knife.

"Come here Teera," he said ominously. "I want to talk to you, I need your help with something."

I dropped the bucket in the well, creating a jarring cacophony as it bounced from wall to wall, falling dozens of feet below ground. I screamed through the noise and ran for the neighbor's house. They were a younger couple, and good friends of ours. They knew me, and they knew Maxie, but they'd never seen this side of him before. They calmed me down and went to see why he was so angry.

They said that when they found him, he was sitting down in the kitchen, crying from remorse. He was wearing shorts, and they noticed three open gashes on one of his thighs, fresh enough that they were still bleeding. He wanted the neighbors to believe that he had cut himself as an act of contrition. It was his way of trying to rectify the situation.

The neighbors took pity on Maxie, and came back to their house to let me know that it was safe to see him. I too felt for Maxie. He looked at me like a child who had just been reprimanded for acting out. Tears still hung in his eyes. I helped him to his feet. The three of us nursed his wounds, and put him to bed.

He didn't get any money from me that day, but it wasn't long before Maxie was in control of my income again. Debt collectors began showing up at the gates to Brown and Company, looking for payment on my husband's accounts. I tried to plead with them, but they threatened me, and they threatened my family.

It's hard to comprehend how debilitating a bout of depression is unless you have gone through one yourself. It's a dark, mind-warping spiral where your brain does not have the physical capacity to function properly. Your sense of self-esteem is completely crushed under a relentless feeling of failure and inevitability. You would like to fight it, but your spirit has no way to muster up the strength. It can seem as though the only way out is to give up. If you have to fight these feelings for long enough, a quick death starts to seem like a clever solution.

My children deserved better than me. They didn't need to hear me weeping at night. They needed their mother to be there for them. They needed the support of someone who had their life in control. They needed a good example to live by, a role model, and I certainly wasn't it.

I came to the conclusion that they would be better off without me, and I began toying with ideas of how to make that so. The thought of killing myself grew appealing as I began to consider how inadequate a parent I had become. My children would be better off if I was gone, and to me at least, that seemed a fact.

I never told Maxie that I was suicidal. I never even told him that I was depressed. He saw that I was withdrawn, but he also thought I that I was cheating on him. He came home drunk one night, screaming that our baby wasn't his. Those words hurt worse than his hands ever did. You can take so many beatings from a man, but that was one of the cruelest things he had ever done to me.

I told him the baby was ours, but he didn't want to believe me. He stumbled closer and began swinging. His punches were slow. He missed completely on the first swing and I moved my head to dodge the second. He had never kicked me before so my eyes didn't look down to see his foot racing towards my stomach.

The kick was off balance, but he put the full force of his weight into it. My body swung around at the waist and I crashed to the floor. His foot shook my upper body and the weight of the blow forced my fragile stomach inward. Terrified that my new child had just been murdered by his own father, I heaved sobs of anger, dripping tiny puddles on a filthy floor.

Maxie left the room as I slowly worked up the courage to rise to my feet. That was the last insult for me. I couldn't take anymore. The abuse wasn't going to stop and my baby was most likely dead anyways. I left the room and took off for the kitchen looking for a can of kerosene.

I hurriedly clutched the silver can and headed out back, unscrewing the cap as I walked. The kerosene initially had a bitter taste as I let it slide down the back of my throat. I gagged on the first sip, but my tongue went numb after that.

My body embraced the liquid and my shoulders seemed to be lifting. I felt euphoric, as though I was flying. The guilt and shame of being unable to care for my own two children, for a moment, seemed like a memory. The child I carried with me, inconsequential. I dropped the can, leaned forward, and vomited on my feet.

Our neighbors ran to the backyard when they heard me heaving and sobbing. I was lying on my side hoping I'd die soon when one of them appeared above me, and sat me upward. She jammed her finger down my throat to make sure I kept vomiting. Her husband fetched water as I slowly expelled every drop of kerosene I had just ingested. Thank God she did, she was the only reason my baby wasn't born without any birth defects.

I lamented in failure as I watched the contents of my stomach pool up on the warm grass beneath me. For months I had thought about suicide, and here I finally mustered the courage to go through with it. I gave my best attempt at ending my life, but apparently even that wasn't enough. Seven months pregnant with my third child, and I was so helpless, I couldn't even manage to kill myself.

Maxie was excited that the baby was on the way; for him, it was an excuse to borrow money from distant relatives. I took care of myself while he started celebrating weeks before the due date. Word reached his father who came to visit us with bottles in hand. The two of them were on a serious binge the day Damian was born. I was amazed I actually made it to the hospital.

I fought rising contractions while squashed in between my husband and his sweaty father in a Morris Minor cab. The two of them spent so much time fumbling over each other that I was well into labor by the time we made it to the car. I tried to fight the pain, but every bump in the road shot an excruciating shockwave up my spine. There was no time for preparation when I eventually made it to the hospital as the baby was crowning right there in the waiting room.

My new baby felt like a weight in my arms. It was the weight of a giant responsibility that I did not think I had the courage for. I had no idea how I was going to feed and raise this child, at least not with Maxie in the picture.

Maxie wasn't in the operating room when Damian was born. He and his father made a scene in the waiting room, claiming to be doctors and demanding to be let in the delivery area. Husbands, at the time, were not allowed in the delivery room. I could hear the two of them arguing with the orderlies as I was wheeled down the hallway. The hospital staff assumed that I was in on the charade and were curt with me both during, and after the procedure.

The situation in the waiting room must have been resolved somehow, because Maxie showed up at my bedside shortly after the doctors let me rest. I handed him his son and he looked back at the child with a smile. Perhaps it was a genuine smile, I couldn't tell. To me it looked as if he was trying to muster up an appropriate reaction.

I had hoped the sight of his own son would be enough to ignite a sense of responsibility within him. But there was no recognition of that fatherly instinct in his eyes. It was at first a smile, and then a blank stare, breaking my heart, and shattering my hopes, our newborn infant resting in his arms.

I couldn't stand it in that hospital. I had to get out. My husband had humiliated me, and there was no use trying to save face with the nurses that worked there. The stark walls and the smell of disinfectant reminded me of my last night with Silva. The hum of florescent lights drove me crazy as I sweltered and brooded atop coarse sheets damp from sweat.

When morning broke, Maxie, the baby, and I dodged the orderlies and quietly slipped out the hospital through a side door. I borrowed ten rupees from our landlady to buy bread and pay the taxi driver. I hadn't eaten anything since the day before so I couldn't yet feed Damian. He had to go hungry until I could feed myself and rest for a short while.

I was foolish to think that things would be different after Damian was born. In fact, they only got worse. Maxie continued to follow me, to accuse me, and to force himself on me. Now that I wasn't pregnant anymore, he had no reason to hold back from all of his old tricks. I was trapped. Having used of the hospitality of everyone else in my family, I called my parents and they took in the kids and me. That way I had somewhere safe to leave the kids so that I could go back to work.

Even though they were eager to help me, I knew that it was nonetheless a burden for my parents to be housing us. When Maxie would harass me, I'd run to the back-yard so my parents couldn't hear us fighting. I knew that having me around was too much for them. I told Maxie I wanted him out of my life. He made it clear that he wouldn't leave me alone as long as I lived. In the time that followed, I moved from house to house in a variety of different towns and neighborhoods and he followed me everywhere I went.

It was past midnight when Maxie came home after a night of drinking. He fumbled over himself in an attempt to woo me into sleeping with him. When I refused he became aggressive. The smell of sweat and stale liquor disgusted me. I was afraid my parents would hear us, so I had no choice but give up the fight. I told myself that this would be the last time I let him do this to me.

After he left in the morning, Mamma came to the kitchen to see me. She said she heard the noises coming from our room, and that the sound kept her awake. I could see her heart breaking for me. I told her that we couldn't let Maxie do this to us anymore, and she agreed.

I grabbed Damian and took off for Marcus' house in Negombo. It took at least 3 hours and 2 buses for us to get there. We were both so tired by the time we arrived that Damian fell asleep in my arms while I carried him from the bus stop to the house.

We stayed there for two days while I tried to figure out our next move. Maxie wouldn't dare touch me in front of Marcus, so I knew I was safe. But I was also a long way from work, and couldn't afford to lose my job for being absent.

Sheila's home in Colombo was much closer to Brown and Company, but I hadn't been allowed to stay there since Maxie and I had taken that awful trip to visit his father in Kandy. Marcus called her, and explained my situation. Sheila and Tony opened up their hearts and allowed Damian and me to stay until we found a more permanent solution.

In my absence Maxie approached several of my family members asking for forgiveness. He cried and begged them to give him another chance. I wasn't surprised when I learned that Maxie had done this, but what I didn't expect was for my family to actually listen to him.

They asked me to at least hear him out. I didn't want to, I was done with him. I told them that I didn't want to listen to him anymore, that I had thought about this from every angle already; that the only thing that I could do was run away. But they convinced me, so to my dismay we contacted Maxie and set up a meeting.

We all met at Mary's home. Sheila, Tony, and Anthony were there. Mary said that day I spoke to Maxie like a lawyer. I explained to him how he had hurt me. I calmly told him that I couldn't take it anymore. She said the words just came out of me as if I had practiced.

We all sat in silence after I had finished. My siblings were shocked; they had never seen me, their little Bubby, be that assertive before. I don't know if they truly understood how bad my relationship had gotten. Maxie sat in the corner like a mouse; he had nothing to say to me.

Of course he apologized, but the words fell on deaf ears. He admitted that he needed help, and pledged to see a psychiatrist. By the time he had finished explaining himself, I agreed to give him another chance. This time, however, I would have conditions for him before I did.

He would have to find work, and a place for us to live. Until he got his act together, I would continue living with

Sheila and Tony. Maxie wouldn't be allowed to live with me until he had met my conditions. He would stay with his family, his friends, or even out on the street. At that point, I didn't care where he went.

Tony used his connections to get Maxie a job at a company named Rowlands. I encouraged Maxie through the process and even brought him lunch during my breaks at Browns. I was actually happy to see my husband working for the first time since I had met him.

He kept asking me to come back to him. I held on to my conviction and told him that we couldn't be together until he had found a place for us to live. Now that he was working, I knew it was possible that he could find a home for us. I had the hope that we could finally start our lives as a happy family. But my hopes were dashed in a little less than 7 days. Maxie quit Rowlands after only one week on the job.

He came to see me after he had quit, but I was so let down. I couldn't even look him in the eye. He wanted me to come with him, and he wanted everything to go back to the way it was, but I couldn't. He made a deal with me, and he broke it. A few days later, he came storming into Sheila and Tony's home, ranting about how unfairly we were treating him.

"You're tearing apart our family!" he screamed.

None of us knew how to react. We tried to appease him, but it only made him angrier. Eventually he walked straight past us and headed for Damian who was watching from the corner.

Tony saw where Maxie was walking and grabbed the child before his father could get to him. Maxie tried to pry him from Tony, but my brother in law held on tight. Sheila and I ran to the three of them and tried to get Maxie to let go of Tony.

We all screamed and eventually Maxie let go. He stepped back and stared at us all in disbelief, his back hunched as if he was going to attack again.

"You're all a bunch of fucking liars!" he screamed. "You said things would go back to normal! You said I could have my family back!"

He stormed out the door before we had a chance to say anything else to him. The three of us fell silent. Damian wailed from Tony's arms. I took the child from Tony and put him to bed. While I was soothing my son, Sheila and Tony began talking about what had just happened.

Their conversation turned into an argument, one that I heard from the next room over. They tried to keep their voices down so that I wouldn't hear them debating about whether or not I should go, but the walls were thin, I understood what they were saying. My presence at their home was more stress than it was worth for them, and I knew that before I even got there.

I couldn't stand the feeling of imposing on my sister. I couldn't stand that my being there was enough to harm her and Tony's relationship. I spent the rest of the night thinking of where I could go next. It was a problem I needed to solve sooner rather than later.

I remember daydreaming that morning, thinking of the different places I could go. I could hide far in the hills of Badulla or near the lagoon in Jaffna. I could find a shack for the kids and me on the beach in Kalmunai. But even as I said it, none of these places seemed far enough away. So long as I was on the island of Sri Lanka, Maxie would find me. I started to think that maybe there really was no way out.

Manel, at Brown and Company, had stayed a good friend of mine over the years. I knew I could always be honest with her. Manel was living in a convent, even though she was a layperson. She was not in any danger, she had no one to hide from, but she was a single, working girl. It wasn't uncommon for girls in her situation to rent a room at a convent. A convent was a safe and uplifting environment to live in. Since her parents lived far away, they saw the convent as a better place for Manel to stay than the YWCA would have been.

Eventually I got the good sense to ask Manel about it. She said that a convent would be just the place for me, and told me all about how it worked. That evening I shared the idea with nearly everyone in my family, and they all were so relieved to know there was another option for me.

I couldn't move in to the convent that Manel was already living in; there wasn't an open room for me. In the following days, we asked around town and researched possible places where I could stay. After a few days of searching, we had a few leads, but nothing that seemed like it would be a good fit.

A few days later, I was at work, just thinking. It was something I did a lot of those days, especially when I was at my desk, while my boss thought my hands were busy. The possibility of moving to a convent, too, was beginning to seem like an illusion. After all my searching, I still had only my prayers, my dreams, and a stack of backed-up paperwork overflowing from the inbox in front of me.

It was just before lunch, and I was dreading the long afternoon that I had in front of me. The phone rang and I answered. The voice on the other end stopped me mid thought. It was a woman's voice, both gentle and comforting. I knew instantly that it wasn't a client, that this woman was calling about something else.

"Teera?" she asked as if the two of us were old friends. "Is this Teera Manatunge?"

I would be lying if I said that I wasn't at least a little bit startled. "Yes, this is Teera," I responded, curious as to what this woman wanted from me.

"Teera, my name is Sister Finbarr. I'm from the Good Shepherd Welcome House, in Borella. How are you?"

"I'm good," I humored her. "What's the Welcome House?"

"The Welcome House is our convent," Sister Finbarr explained. "There are five or so of us sisters living here and several laywomen staying with us. All of them need a safe place where they can rest their heads."

"Teera," she went on, "your information was given to us from someone in your family. I know that they love you very much. They mentioned that you might have fallen on hard times."

"Who told you that?" I said

"That person, for now, wishes to remain anonymous. But I can assure you, he or she is very close to you," she said.

I figured it must have been Sheila. I don't know how she met Sister Finbarr, but the opportunity was so exciting, I wanted to jump through the phone. I still didn't know how to react, so I kept the conversation moving, "Ok," I said cautiously, "what do I have to do?"

"I'd like you to come down to the convent today after work. Come see the facility. We can talk about your family, and maybe about how the Welcome House can help you through this time in your life."

Any malaise that I was feeling before that conversation went right out the window when I hung up the phone. I turned to my stack of paperwork, dove in, and got everything done so that I could leave a few minutes early that day. When it was time to go, I grabbed my things, called to check in on the kids, and hopped on a bus to Borella. The Welcome House was only a short walk from where the bus dropped me off.

A tall, cinderblock wall protected the complex on all four sides, with an intimidating gate that was studded at the top to prevent intruders from climbing over. I carefully approached the facility, unsure of how to get in. Past the gate, a short verandah led to a quaint, white, two-story convent. Clean and freshly painted, the building looked angelic.

I stood there, admiring the building for a moment, when the front doors opened and she emerged and walked confidently toward me. Sister Finbarr was the epitome of an Irish nun. Despite her pallor and gentle diction, she had a commanding, motherly presence about her. I never knew what color her hair was because she always kept it in a habit.

She opened the gate and began showing me around. The Welcome House was home to about a dozen women from broken homes in the surrounding area. The high walls around the complex kept out intruders, and visitors were only allowed in with permission.

We entered in through the front door where there was a waiting room and an administrative office. Adjacent to the office was a multipurpose room. Behind a door and down the hall were a few living quarters, a chapel, a kitchen, and a nursery for orphaned children. At the end of the hall was a set of stairs; on the second floor there were six more rooms that slept both staff and guests.

Sister Finbarr explained that the goal of the Welcome House was to not only provide shelter to women who need it, but to also provide counseling and spiritual guidance.

She said they had an open room for me, but unfortunately I wouldn't be allowed to have my children stay with me. The Welcome House was limited in resources and therefore could only offer so much hospitality. If I were to take Sister Finbarr up on her offer, I would have to do it alone. Without much hesitation, I quietly made arrangements for the kids to stay with my family, and moved in to the Welcome House the next day.

For the first time in months, I spent the night peacefully. The rush of returning to work well rested was a feeling I hadn't experienced since Chandra and I were together. That night I returned to the Welcome House and used the facility as my home base. After dinner I would talk with Sister Finbarr and we slowly went through the details of everything that happened to me, starting with when I was a little girl.

Sister Finbarr listened to me. She heard my story without any sort of intention or judgment. In the following days, she gave me some simple suggestions for helping myself, and my perspective on life began to change drastically. After only a few days and nights at the Welcome House, I found myself smiling again.

There was no doubt that I was making progress. I felt strong and confident. Maybe I was getting ahead of myself, but it didn't seem like it would be long before I became strong enough to leave Maxie. The closer I became to Sister Finbarr, the more I hoped that she would be able to help me plan my escape.

I brought up the idea in one of our counseling sessions. I told her that I needed to get away from him; that it didn't matter if I divorced him or not, I just needed to get away, permanently. I certainly thought that she would support the idea, but she looked back at me with confusion instead.

"Teera," she said. "You still don't know who from your family sent you here, do you?"

"I was actually wondering that myself," I said. "I mean I figured it was one of my sisters. They can't stand that man. They've been trying to pry me away from him since the beginning."

"I see," Sister Finbarr said. "Do you think sometimes you may be trying to escape your marriage?"

"Of course! That's why I'm here, right?"

"What I mean to say is," Sister Finbarr went on, "do you think that you're trying to find a way out because marriage was harder than you thought it would be? That maybe you haven't tried to save this marriage yet, and that's why it feels like it's not working?"

"How can I try, Sister? After what that man has done to me? What else is there to save?"

"Maxie seems to see it differently," she said.

"You've been talking to him?"

"Teera," Sister Finbarr said, "Maxie was the one that gave us your name. He asked us to reach out to you. Teera, I know that he loves you very much, and that with enough prayer and time, I think we all know that you two can make things work."

"Maxie?" I blurted out, "but why would he send me here? He knows I'm trying to leave him."

"He told us that you were trying to leave him, but he's trying to stop you," she said. "By marrying this man you made a vow before God. Teera, you have to honor that vow."

"But you don't understand," I objected.

"Teera," she said with authority, "We have been speaking with Maxie and we know he's a good husband. He told us all about how your sisters want you to leave him. But I know you can prove them wrong. The two of you just need to work things out."

"Work things out?" I was devastated. "How can I work things out with him? My children can't live under one roof because of him!"

"But you have to *try* to save this marriage," she said. "As a sister of The Lord I can't simply let you run away from this man. Starting tomorrow, he will be coming here every evening so that the two of you can begin talking."

"But there's nothing to work out!" I said.

"Maxie doesn't seem to see it that way," Sister Finbarr said. "And neither do I. If you want to continue living at the Welcome House, you *will* make amends with your husband. It's right for you, and it's right for your family. Teera, it's what God wants for you."

The Welcome House was supposed to be my escape from Maxie. I was supposed to be alone. I wasn't supposed to be afraid at night anymore. Instead Maxie had me right where he wanted me. He knew exactly where I was living, he knew where all the kids were, and he had the whole staff of this convent on his side.

I spent that night trying to think of ways I could escape and make it on my own. But that would have put me right back where I started. I had no choice but to stay there and face him.

He would show up at the same time every evening, apologetic and looking like God's gift to Catholic women across the world. The nuns ate up his feigned sense of devotion and became convinced that my marriage was one worth saving. I sat through my sessions with him, bored and unresponsive. I knew that I was never going to see a change in Maxie, so why even try? My efforts appeased the Sisters, but I knew this couldn't last for long.

I started lengthening my walks home from work to avoid having to spend time with him. For hours I would circle blocks and trudge through dark streets until I eventually got tired and had to return to the convent. Sure enough, Maxie would always be waiting for me with one of the nuns, sipping tea and seeking advice on how to change my mind.

He spent so much time trying to trap me, why couldn't he have spent his energy getting himself together? At one point I sincerely thought about the idea of trying to make it work with him. I thought maybe he would come around, or I would be able to stand it at some point. But I could never let myself. There were too many things he had already done to me that were too hard to overlook.

Even though I still had to see Maxie every day, he wasn't in a position where he could hurt me anymore. And that was enough to help me through those painful evenings. Every day I grew stronger, and with that strength, I planned to go somewhere far enough where Maxie could never see me again.

He didn't know it, but Maxie's plan to trap me in the Welcome House was slowly backfiring. I was getting ready to make my move, and was gaining my independence right under his nose. At night I kept dreaming of ways to run away and hoped that my chance would be coming soon. I just had to make sure that from now on, I always stayed one step ahead of him.

It didn't take long for the Sisters at the Welcome House to catch on to the idea that Maxie was conning them. The inconsistencies in his stories started to add up. Besides that, I remained persistent with the counselor I was assigned to, a Sister named Mavis Perrera. Maxie would tell stories at the convent, and I would separate fact from fiction in my private sessions with Mavis.

She was able to convince Sister Finbarr that Maxie was not to be trusted. Once we had won over Sister Finbarr, that was the end of it, Maxie wasn't allowed past the gate anymore. He would still show up and wait by the gate from time to time, hoping that he would catch me walking alone.

With Maxie kept at bay, I was able to really start working on resolving my issues. We started all the way back from when I was a little girl, and one by one addressed all of the insecurities and mental scars that I had been carrying with me for years. She taught me to forgive myself, and to trust in God again. Mavis had lost her husband to a heart attack, so she, better than anyone, could relate to where I was coming from.

When I addressed my problems, and regained my faith, it was amazing how much happier and 'in control' I felt. I began communicating with people more often. I found myself less ashamed of the mark that I wore on my face. In time, I came to open up to the other women that were living around me. Relative to their stories, my problems seemed comparable, if not less tragic. They too, were all forced to run from their homes. I always knew I wasn't the only one, but I had never met anyone, let alone a whole group of women, that could truly relate to me.

After some time, they began to confide in me, and I put my trust in them. Those women reminded me of how much I was truly blessed with. They gave me the courage to turn a corner and face each day with a sense of gratitude. Gratitude turned into hope and I prayed that one day soon I could have my own home where I could live with my children in peace. It was not too much to ask for. But for the first time in my life, I actually believed that it could happen.

I still remember the night that things began turning around. I was returning to my room late, after dinner, when I paused to notice the sounds of crying children in the nursery. In the doorway I found Sister Finbarr, gently cradling one of the infants to try and lull him to sleep. As I drew closer I noticed five more orphaned infants in cradles around the room, including one that was in a fit of tears.

I carefully approached the crib and gently rocked the child in my arms. Almost instantly, the infant curled back into sleep and the nursery became noticeably quiet. Sister Finbarr glanced back at me with a look of relief that I had not yet seen in such a strong woman as herself. The constant task of caring for the battered women at the Welcome House was responsibility enough for anyone. Combine that with the challenge of raising six small, orphaned children, and I'm not sure if she ever slept.

It was almost midnight, and as we were both returning to our rooms, Sr. Finbarr stopped by the staircase. She smiled at me and said, "Teera, you are one of us, why didn't you become a nun?"

The comment surprised me; the idea never crossed my mind. "Oh Sister," I said. "I don't have the discipline to be a nun. I don't think I could ever do what you do."

She smiled. We both climbed the stairs together and went to our rooms. I was honored she felt that way about me. Helping Sister Finbarr put the infants to sleep would become my nightly task in the weeks that followed. It was a way of giving back to the nuns that had given me so much. Putting the infants to bed was something that made me feel good, and something I looked forward to every time the sun set.

But with each child that I cradled, I could not help but think about the three that belonged to me. I longed to be with them more than anything. I prayed to God that He look over them. I prayed that someday I could be with my children just like any mother should. I prayed that the Lord be with the orphaned children in that nursery, and all of the shattered souls that sought refuge in the gentle care of the Welcome House.

That Saturday I was visiting Shirlene and Damian at my sister Mary's home. Jude, at the time, was staying with Sheila and Tony. As I approached the house, I could hear Damian crying from outside. My blood curdled when I heard his familiar scream. I hurried up to the house and nearly fainted when I let myself in the front door.

When I walked in, Mary was swinging the end of the cane at my baby while he moved from side to side, failing to dodge her blows. Shirlene was watching from the couch, her face pale and damp with tears, her limbs rigid, too scared to move or say anything.

Damian was disturbed when he was a child. Because of the circumstances he was born into, he was often neglected, and cried uncontrollably because of it. Mary found it hard to sympathize with a child that was as difficult to appease as Damian was.

Her home was always pristine, neat and quiet. She was the sister that always seemed to "have it all together." Mary had two children; one was a boy, who had already moved out of her home and was working as an inspector for the police. The other was a little girl, about ten years old, who hardly spoke.

She had finally broken that day. Beating Damian with a cane was the only thing she could think to do to stop him from crying. The more he screamed, the harder she hit him. She didn't stop as I entered the room. I would never forget the sound of my little boy wailing over Mary cursing under her breath, the cane she found slapping and popping against the soft skin and tender bones of a harmless toddler.

I screamed at Mary to stop, and she did. She turned to me and began to explain why she needed to cane Damian. It wasn't uncommon for children to be beaten in those days, but not like this, not by their aunts. Without hesitation, I grabbed Damian and attempted to leave. I grabbed Shirlene by the hand on my way out.

"Come on baby," I said to my daughter, "let's get you out of here."

I was almost to the door when Mary stopped me.

"Leave Shirlene with me," she pleaded.

At first I didn't listen.

"Take Damian," she said, "he's better off with you, but leave Shirlene. Think about this rationally, Bubby, where are you going to take the two of them?"

I choked up when I realized that she was right. I couldn't go back to the Welcome House, not with my children with me. Now that Damian couldn't stay at Mary's anymore, I was back to square one; I didn't have anywhere to go.

Regrettably I left Shirlene at Mary's and took to the streets with Damian, looking for a room to rent. After some searching, I found a home with a sign in front that said 'Room for Rent.' A pleasant lady in a sari answered the door. Her name was Mrs. Jawardena, and she took a liking to Damian and me. The rent was affordable, and Mrs. Jawardena was willing to let me move in that day.

She had three children, two teenaged daughters and an eldest son that was twenty years old. I explained my situation with Maxie to Mrs. Jawardena, and she was willing to let Damian and me stay anyway. The four of them were all very kind, they showed us to our bed, and gave us everything we needed for the evening.

I left Damian at Mrs. Jawardena's and went back to the Welcome House to tell Sister Finbarr what had happened. She looked concerned when I told her that I would be moving out of the convent. She urged me not to leave, but my mind was made up. I gathered the few things that I had in my room and made my way to the gate.

"Teera," Sister Finbarr said before I left, "I want you to remember that the doors of the Welcome House are always open to you."

The next day, Maxie was waiting for me after work. He followed me home, and decided that he would move in with us. Maxie tried to use his charm on Mrs. Jawardena, but he couldn't fool her, and he couldn't fool the kids. I had already warned them about Maxie, and they remained skeptical, even as he began spending the night there.

Mrs. Jawardena, too, had been widowed when she was younger, forced to raise her three children alone. She understood where I was coming from, and the whole family took us under their wing. Maxie wouldn't dare harm me with them around.

More importantly, the family helped take care of Damian during the day so that I could go to work. Each evening I would come home, and they would have Damian all dressed up and waiting for me on the verandah. We lived in that home for about six months, and in that time, he never cried for attention. He was quiet and content, adequately fed, and in the auspices of a home that was filled with love.

I wanted more than anything to have Shirlene live with us there, but I also couldn't bear the thought of my beautiful and timid little girl having to share a bedroom with her alcoholic stepfather. Even though I couldn't have her with me, I knew that Shirlene was safe with Mary.

Jude had been living at Sheila's home, but we had to think of a new plan when Sheila and her husband decided to move to Nigeria for work. Around the same time, Maxie had gone missing for a few days. We learned that he had been thrown in jail for impersonating a doctor. With him locked up for the time being, I figured that it was safe for me to take Jude, and move back in with my parents.

I was grateful that my parents could take us in again, but it was hard seeing them in their elder years. My father was beginning to lose his eyesight, and my mother was starting to look weak. We all took care of each other in those first few days. We got to be re-united in peace. I spent time with my parents, and we all spent time with the children.

I was only there for a few days before Maxie showed up at the doorstep again. I didn't know that he had gotten out of jail. He would show up at the window from time to time, apologize, and ask me to take him back. I would give him reasons as to why I couldn't take him back, and the discussion always ended up in a fight. He wouldn't leave until we were yelling at each other.

One night he showed up at our door bleeding from his face. He looked like he had gotten beaten badly. We took him in, cleaned his wounds, fixed his shirt, and let him sleep in the guest's bed since it was late. In the morning, my parents and I made him breakfast.

Before he left, he called me close to him, "Teera, I have to tell you something," he said. I crossed the room and leaned in thinking that he was going to thank me. He slapped me instead, and ran out the front door.

That week, with her permission, I sent divorce papers to Maxie's sister's house. Maxie refused to sign them when his sister presented them to him. He claimed that he couldn't divorce me because the Bible forbade it.

A few days passed before I saw him again. It was on a casual afternoon when I was walking home from work. I saw his familiar figure waiting for me on the sidewalk. As I drew closer, the outline became clearer, and my head drooped when I recognized his familiar stumble. It was broad daylight; Maxie was drunk, screaming at me from behind sunken eyes.

"Where have you been, Teera?" He demanded, yelling loud enough for onlookers to take notice.

He looked scary that day, and from the moment I saw him I knew that it was going to be a long evening. Rather than taking the bus home, I decided to go to the Welcome House instead. I began rushing toward the convent when he pulled me back by the arm and said, "You better not run. If you do, I'll pull your sari off."

I knew he meant it, but I started running as fast as I could anyways.

"Come back here, Teera! I want to talk to you!" He grabbed my shoulder. "I know why you haven't been coming back at night! I know what's wrong!"

"Nothing's wrong Maxie!" I said. "Get away from me!" People gathered to watch the two of us argue.

"You've been sleeping with someone else haven't you? Admit it!" Maxie screamed and the people in the crowd started whispering.

"No Maxie! I swear!" I tried to save face in front of the group of strangers.

"Stop lying damn it!"

Maxie slapped me hard enough that I spun to the ground. The crowd gasped. I heard a man yell to Maxie, "That's right! Give the woman something to think about!"

Maxie struck me twice more while I was on the ground, now bantering to the reactions of the audience. I cried for help but no one wanted to listen; they all figured that I was getting what was coming to me. I finally made it to my feet and ran towards the convent, but Maxie took off after me. My sandals and sari slowed my stride and I struggled to gain speed, my soles clacking loudly down the street.

He caught up to me in front of the All Saints Church, where he grabbed the back of my neck and repeatedly hit me in front of the door to the chapel. I screamed for help but people just stared. I tried to run but Maxie grabbed my sari and started pulling so as to undress me in public. He wanted people to see him beat me. He wanted me humiliated and bruised in public so that no one else would ever want me. I prayed for a miracle, even death, anything to end the pain and take me away from that shameful sidewalk.

Maxie grabbed my hair so he could drag me off like a helpless dog when a van sped closer and stopped right next to us. The two of us stopped and looked up to see my brother, Marcus, and two of his friends getting out. The three of them opened their doors and charged toward Maxie. Marcus grabbed a cricket bat from some small children and began swinging for Maxie who immediately let go of my head and took off running.

It was the first time I had ever seen Maxie scared. I didn't want Marcus to hurt him. My husband wasn't worth it. I chased after the two of them and grabbed Marcus' arm before he had a chance to make contact with Maxie. My husband ran off and Marcus took me back to his van. I heard cheers as the crowd slowly dispersed, but I was just glad to be safe. Marcus screamed at Maxie. "You bloody bastard! If you touch my sister again I'll kill you!"

It was a miracle that Marcus' showed up that day to save me. At the time he lived in Negombo, nearly 50 miles away. He happened to be in Borella that day, and he happened to be on the right street at the right time.

The Welcome House was only a few hundred yards away, so when the sisters heard the commotion, they called the police. The officers arrived shortly after Marcus pulled me away from Maxie. He continued to muse about the situation, even as he was being arrested. To Maxie, the incident was a big joke, something he was proud of. We could hear him cackling like a demon from the back seat of the police car. Confident that Maxie was in jail for the night, Marcus drove me to my parents' home to rest for the evening.

My mother and I settled down to an uneasy breakfast. She sadly looked in my eyes and asked me to tell her everything that happened the day before. My eyes welled up. I began to recount the story when my sentence was cut short by a voice coming from the window. I knew who it was, and the sound shot daggers through my heart.

"Teera!" it said. "Teera, over here!"

Maxie was tapping on the window, trying to get our attention. He looked like a vagrant from his long night in jail. His face was filthy and his hair smelled rotten. His eyes were bloodshot and he wasn't making any sense.

"Teera," he said. "I'm so sorry for what I did to you. I didn't mean it, I don't know what happened. I love you! Please forgive me! I swear I'll never hurt you again!"

Of course his apologies didn't mean anything to me, but more than that I was scared. I didn't know how long this apologetic façade would last, and I knew I had to get out of his sight before his charming side wore off. I let my mother keep him busy while I snuck out the back door, hopped the wall, and headed straight for the Welcome House. I asked the Sisters to keep me there until we could come up with a new plan.

I have often found hope hard to come by. It is not the sort of commodity that just appears in places that you would expect to find it. An ideal that I had never completely abandoned, hope, at one time, had become a long forgotten feeling for me.

I had been in and out of the Welcome House for about five years. Typically the girls that stayed there would find a solution for themselves within about a year. A lot of them went to the Middle East where there were plenty of opportunities for them to work as nannies.

For me, the Middle East was out of the question. I would not have been able to bring the children with me. It seemed there was no other solution for me, and I couldn't understand why.

I felt like time was running out. My children were growing up without me. Each night I spent away from them was another night where I missed the chance to see them grow up. I could never get those nights back, and I couldn't stand to waste any more of them.

I was prepared to do anything, but for the time being I had very little to place my hopes on. As it so often goes, when I stopped searching, hope found me. It found me in the form of a letter to my family, from a long-lost brother, who had moved to the United States years before. The letter bore the promise of a visit. A visit that, unbeknownst to me, would catalyze an answer to my prayers.

My older brother, Cyril, had sent a letter to the family promising to visit us in Sri Lanka. We had not heard from Cyril in over twenty-five years and the letter was a surprising yet welcome recount of troubles abroad and memories of home. He talked about everyone in our family: brothers, sisters, parents, everyone that is…except for me.

Cyril never knew me. He knew *of* me, but we had never lived under the same roof together. By the time I was born, he had already moved out and later, joined the Royal Navy. He traveled the world while serving, and then chose to settle in the United States with his family when his stint in the military had ended.

Eager to get to know Cyril, I wrote him back, shaming him for forgetting me. It had been so long since he had been to Sri Lanka, I told him that the entire family and I would love to see him. I even offered to show him around the island if he ever made it out.

To our surprise, Cyril wrote back only a short while later. He told us that he had booked tickets for a flight back home, and that we should expect to see him in a matter of weeks. When he finally arrived, the family took him in; we made a big meal, and he regaled us with stories from the USA.

Cyril wanted to take me up on my offer to show him around, to be his "tour guide" as he called it. I couldn't help but say yes, and took a few days off work so that we could go exploring. We saw my favorite beaches and my favorite parts of town. I even took him to some of the more touristy sites just for the heck of it, and through our little daytime adventures the two of us became much closer.

Cyril eventually went back to the U.S., and I didn't know when I would be seeing him again. There was talk amongst my family, while he was in Sri Lanka, of Cyril sponsoring my immigration to the United States. I couldn't say that I was opposed to the idea. But I also didn't want to get my hopes up. I had become accustomed to disappointments. The idea of one day jumping on a plane and starting my life over in America, to me at least, seemed far-fetched.

The process would take time and money, forms and background checks. It would be a big commitment for Cyril, and an even bigger commitment for me. Cyril had his own family and job to think about. I found it hard to believe that he would be able to take the time out to do this for me.

That's probably the reason why I didn't know how to react when he wrote to tell me that he wanted to do it. He wanted me to come live with him in California until I could afford a home of my own. He'd sponsor my immigration, and we would go through the process together. I remember feeling so happy, but also scared, and yet brave at the same time. I was just overjoyed. I really didn't know how to react.

I felt very privileged to have Cyril as my sponsor. The immigration process was almost impossible to get through unless you had someone from the U.S. sponsoring you. The U.S. government was very selective about the immigrants that they chose to let through. Those who applied alone were often denied a visa, resulting in a great deal of lost money and wasted effort.

Cyril did have one condition before he signed off on his end: the divorce with Maxie had to be final. There could not be any baggage attached to me as I went through the immigration paperwork. It would have been a waste for both of us if I went through the entire process only to be denied immigration because my husband had a criminal record.

The timing worked out because Maxie happened to be back in jail. He called me and asked if I would bring him supplies. I came to visit him, and I took Sister Bernadette from the Welcome House with me. I brought him a few things that I knew he would need for the next few days. But I also brought him our divorce papers, and he reluctantly signed them from behind steel bars.

I never thought I would see the day, but my divorce with Maxie was signed, stamped, and declared final on Damian's ninth birthday. With the sisters from the Welcome House by my side, I made a good showing in court and gained custody of our son.

Maxie put on a show at the hearing. He was out of jail by then, so he arrived at the courthouse clean cut and ready to talk his way through anything. The judge gave him no sympathy and Maxie didn't seem to be surprised. His criminal record was enough to overshadow any kind of performance he might have been able to put on for the judge.

That evening I attended the Novena at the All Saints Church with Damian. We didn't know it, but Maxie was waiting for us outside. We saw him while exiting the church with the congregation after service. He was holding a birthday cake and said that he came to celebrate Damian's birthday. Damian, of course wanted to eat cake with his father, but instead I grabbed him by the hand and ran down the street to the Welcome House.

He followed us all the way there. "Teera!" he said as I closed the gate on him. "Divorce means nothing to me, I'm never going to leave you alone…"

My biggest hurdle before leaving Sri Lanka would be ensuring that my children had safe places to stay. They couldn't come to America with me, not yet at least. I would have to get on my feet first. Then I would be able to sponsor their immigration.

I sent Shirlene to live with Sheila and her husband. They were living in Nigeria at the time, and I was able to send Shirlene back with them when they came to Sri Lanka for holiday. It was a tough decision, but I had to let her go. It meant that once I left the country, my family would be spread over three continents. The logistics of sending my daughter that far away from home were frightening for me but I could rest assured that Sheila would be taking care of her.

Damian was already staying in a boarding school that I had regrettably put him some years before. I was having trouble keeping Damian at school. Maxie would often visit him there. On the nights where Maxie was too drunk to get himself home, he would sleep in Damian's room.

I hated having to leave him there. He was still little, only nine years old. He had been going there since he was six. He must have been so confused as to why he couldn't live with his mamma, or his siblings. It felt like we were sending him off to prison.

It didn't matter how good of a child he was, we still had to send him off because there were no other options. There was no way we could explain the situation so that it would make sense to him. I couldn't stand how much he hated that school. And I made a promise to myself that I would send for him, my little Damian whom I already missed, the very first chance that I got.

Jude joined a novitiate a few months before Cyril came to visit. He studied to be a priest but his ambitions were short lived, so I enrolled him in St. Benedict's boarding school with Damian. I was so relieved to see the two of them together.

Damian needed his older brother. He needed an example, and he needed the love of his big brother. He needed someone to look after him, and to help him understand why we all couldn't be together. Damian needed Jude so that he could learn to trust his family again, so that he could learn to grow up without harboring a deep animosity for all of us.

With my two boys and my only daughter all in safe hands, I could rest assured that my children were taken care of. Every day I prepared for my departure. I arranged things to pack, organized my finances and made sure I had enough money to live comfortably until I made it to The States. My friends helped me sift through the hoards of paperwork that it took to secure my visa.

My last day at work was an emotional mess of well wishing and fond reminiscing. The staff at Brown and Company had become part of my family over the last few years and all of them knew the turmoil I was facing at home. After feeling like such an outcast when I first joined the company, I had grown close with all of them. They no longer felt like strangers, these people were my friends.

The staff threw me a farewell party, complete with speeches from co-workers and bosses. At the end I was given a gift. With the gift was a list of people who contributed to it, and the amount that each person put towards the present. I was surprised at the generosity of my co-workers, but one name, at the very bottom of the list, particularly touched my heart. Our janitor, Sanjeev, contributed one rupee. It was the least that one could possibly give, and all that he could afford. It meant more to me than all of the other donations combined.

I was asked to give a speech before the event ended. Despite my best efforts I found that there were no words to describe the sense of gratitude and love I felt towards my friends and co-workers. These people had become a source of strength for me. They aided me through my darkest moments, providing the confident reassurance that I will, in fact, make it through. Unable to say anything more, I offered a simple and sincere, "thank you." There was nothing more that I could say to them, but the words had never seemed more genuine.

Maxie had been thrown back in jail as I was making preparations for my move. It was a convenient break to not have him stalking me around town, especially as word of my departure spread from person to person. He was released a few days before I left and sought me out with a look of sadness in his eyes.

"What a waste," I thought to myself.

He looked sick and broken. I gave him twenty rupees, danced around the subject of my departure, and left him with an empty promise to visit shortly. Behind his back, I made arrangements to have Maxie's sister occupy him the day I left. It was uncomfortable for me to be dishonest with someone, even him, but he left me no choice, and I wasn't intimidated by him anymore.

When the day finally came, I took the bus to my parents' house, went back to Borella for Novena with my family, and rode in a long caravan to the airport. I said my goodbyes and stepped timidly through the airport. Inching closer towards a new life for myself, each step was a bittersweet leap of hope and achievement. After so many years of praying for some sort of reprieve from my misery, the day had actually come.

One of my co-workers at Brown & Company arranged for an article to be written about me in the daily newspaper;

it ran the day after I left. The headline read, "Teera Off to California." Maxie apparently stormed off in a fit of rage when he saw it. He came to my parents' house looking for answers, but it was too late. I was already gone, and there was absolutely nothing he could do about it.

17ᵗʰ June 1980. It was my first time out of the country and my second time on an airplane. I gazed out my window as the captain made ready for take off.

I said to myself, "Maxie, you can't catch me anymore now, can you?"

I smiled as I thought about how dumbfounded he would be when he found out that I was gone. The woman he thought he had under his thumb suddenly disappears, vanishing to America without even leaving a note.

My heart raced as the massive airliner gained altitude and my worries became more distant. This would be the farthest from home I had ever traveled. There would be a whole new set of challenges ahead of me. But a new chapter in my life was indeed beginning and I felt as though God was present in literally every step I took.

The Lord brought me from the depths of self-loathing to a hopeful future where my dreams were within reach. After so many years of struggle, it was hard to believe that I had come this far, but in my heart, I knew I was ready.

It was as if He were sitting next to me on my flight that evening, comforting me as I quietly let go of my burdens back in Sri Lanka. My new life was ahead of me, and as relieving as I knew that would be, my work was still not done. I prayed that God be with my children as

I left them behind to find solace in a new home for all four of us.

The hours crawled by before the staggering urban mass of Los Angeles came into view beneath my tiny passenger window. "This is the land of freedom and opportunity," I thought as I gazed upon the vast expanse of homes and buildings.

I could be anything I wanted to here, and finally that freedom was available to me. It reminded me of when God parted the Red Sea. It was as if the Lord had taken the unbearable forces that were holding me back, and drove them apart to let me find peace in this new land.

I was prepared for the culture shock; Cyril warned me that people in the U.S. move a lot faster than people in Sri Lanka do. I had barely stepped off the plane when I was whisked into a hustling hoard of travelers bound for customs. I struggled to gather my belongings as one stranger after another brushed passed me to secure a place in the security queue. By the time I made it to the checkpoint, I was exhausted, my hands full, and dead last in line.

I stopped for a moment to catch my breath and collect myself. The process seemed like it would take a long time. I watched the people in front of me. When you got to the front of the line, you had to show your paperwork. The customs officers asked you a few questions, and then you were instructed to sit down and wait to be cleared before you could leave.

By the time I got to the front of the line, no one had left yet. All the seats in the waiting area were filled as frustrated travelers listened anxiously for their names to be called. I uneasily stepped forward, and the officer greeted me with a stony stare.

"Passport please," he said blankly.

I gave him my passport, and fumbled with my stack of other paperwork, which included forms, photos and a set of X-rays. He took a picture for my green card, asked me a few more questions, and again stared at me inquisitively.

After a pause he stamped my passport, smiled, and said, "we noticed you getting pushed to the end of the line back there."

The officer caught me off guard.

"We didn't like seeing that happen," he said. "We didn't think it was fair. So since you were the last person in line to show your paperwork, we think you should be the first person to get cleared to leave."

The officer laughed with another man he was working with, and handed back my passport. The two of them looked back to a window where two more customs agents were grinning and waving.

"Everything checked out, you can go ahead and claim your baggage. We'll start letting everyone else here leave in a minute." He paused and smiled. "Welcome to the United States, Ms. Fonseka," the officer said. "Enjoy your new home."

I wanted to pinch myself. I was walking on clouds as I made my way though the terminal and toward the lobby. Cyril was waiting with a camera, ready to take my picture. Before that day I was terrified of the idea of staring down a camera lens. At moments like this, I had become accustomed to straying away from attention, hiding my appearance to avoid potential embarrassment. I was tired of hiding my face and instead embraced the moment. I smiled big, and let him snap the camera.

"There she is!" Cyril exclaimed. "The sister that I forgot existed. The only one that's managed to come to America, after all these years."

The drive to Cyril's house from the airport was overwhelming. The buildings, the traffic, the strange people wandering up and down the street swirled together to create a kaleidoscope of sight and sound that assaulted my weary senses. I suddenly felt so small as we sat in traffic on the enormous 405 Freeway, with its masses of angry drivers and flashy cars. It was frightening and exciting all at the same time. My stomach swirled as I took in the cityscape and dreamed of how I might find a niche for myself in this sprawling metropolis.

Cyril lived in a town called Lancaster, which was outside of the city. That night Cyril prepared a magnificent Sri Lankan dinner for us. He was always a really great cook. The spices reminded me of the home I had just left behind. We talked late into the night and shared stories about our siblings and our parents. He was the eldest in the family, and I was the youngest, meaning our perspectives on growing up at home were always quite different.

My brother was confident that I would be able to strike it out on my own and spent a good part of the night reassuring my doubts. I would like to say I was thoroughly brave throughout the process of this move, but I was not. Some one close helped me through every step of the way.

I spent a lot of time in the first few days adjusting to life in a big city while simultaneously getting over a bout of jet lag for the first time in my life. I was constantly marveling at the different amenities in Cyril's house that to him seemed commonplace, like hot showers and non-stick pans.

I fumbled through tasks around the kitchen and found myself baffled by nearly all of his appliances. I was trying to be a helpful sister, but I just ended up getting in the way. Cyril teased me about how new I was to everything, and about how bad my cooking was. He tried to give me a few household pointers, but for those first few weeks, I was pretty much helpless.

Sheila called from Nigeria to congratulate me for making it to the U.S. in one piece. It was good to hear from her, but it was better to hear from my daughter. The three of us caught up. I told them about how big and exciting the United States was. Sheila and Shirlene were both enthralled with my stories, but all I wanted to do was see them again.

"When's the next time we're all going to be together?" I asked my sister in Sinhala, hoping there would be some sort of occasion in the near future.

"There won't be an occasion for quite a long time, Bubby, unless you're planning to come back to Sri Lanka for Christmas this year," Sheila said.

"I wish I could," I said.

"So what then?" I asked Sheila.

I figured there had to be another option, but I was all out of ideas.

"Well," Sheila paused for a moment. "What if I came and visited with the girls?" By 'the girls' Sheila meant Shirlene and her own daughter, Anne.

"Sheila!" I didn't know what else to say. "I would love that! When can you get here?"

Sheila took to booking their flights. The three of them would arrive in a matter of weeks. I was so excited to see them I could hardly contain myself.

The day of their flight Cyril and I cleaned the house until it was spotless. We were too tired to cook, so he ordered pizza for lunch. It was the first time I had eaten pizza. That evening we drove to LAX to pick the three of them up. I couldn't wait to see my precious, little girl. She had gotten taller since the last time I had seen her. She was beautiful and glowing. I couldn't wait to touch her.

We gave each other a long hug, and from the moment that she met them, Shirlene had won over every member of Cyril's family. They adored my charming daughter, and in the days that followed, we had a wonderful time together. We rode bicycles almost every evening as far was we could go.

I took her shopping at Kmart one day; we were both going through the sale racks. We had split up so that we could each find what we were looking for. When we both met at the cash register, we looked at each other's hands to see that we had both picked out the exact same dress.

We both laughed, I put mine back on the rack, and paid for the one that Shirlene was holding. It warmed my heart to know that despite the distance between us, my daughter still had the same taste as me.

Shirlene also went with me to my first cleaning job. By the end of it, we were so tired that we had both lost our appetites. The job was way more than I had bargained for, and I was so grateful that she had volunteered to go with me to help.

Shirlene and I never discussed living conditions for the future. We were just enjoying our time together. Sheila and Cyril took it upon themselves to make the decisions as to what would happen when Sheila's trip to America came to a close.

The two of them had decided to let Anne stay with Cyril so that she could attend college in Antelope Valley. She had already applied for a student visa, so legally she was allowed to stay. Since I still did not have a job or a home of my own, I had no choice but to send Shirlene back to Nigeria with Sheila.

I was devastated when I had to put her back on that plane, and I didn't know what to do. Cyril suggested that I go to community college so that I could learn the American way. I needed to learn how to use more sophisticated machines like typewriters and calculators. That kind of experience, he said, would help me get a good job, so that I could find a home for myself. Once I had a job and a home, I could apply for my children's immigration.

For a while it seemed like the task of finding a job and getting on my feet would be impossible to accomplish. I was in an enormous city with different customs. My scar instantly stood out to potential employers, and most certainly did not help my chances for getting hired. Sure I had administrative experience working for Brown and Company, but in the states, that experience gave me only so much credibility.

My feelings of anxiety and inadequacy held me back for a long time. I needed work so badly, that it was hard not to come off as desperate during interviews. For about four months, I bounced around to all sorts of different odd jobs, from housekeeping to hospice care. Cyril advised me not to take these jobs, but I had to start somewhere. The way I saw it, I had no time to waste. Because of that, I became easy prey for those who were looking for cheap labor. I was worked to the bone, and paid a pittance for it.

At one point I met a friend of Cyril's named Liza at the bowling alley by our house. She offered me a job helping her care for four mentally ill patients at her home. Liza said she would pay me five hundred dollars a month for the work. My hours would be from 8am to 8pm, six days a week.

At the end of my first month, Liza went back on our original agreement and told me that she could only pay me two hundred dollars a month. Cyril was furious, and told me that I should quit immediately. I told him that two hundred dollars a month was better than making nothing at all. As soon as I found something better, I'd quit the job with Liza.

Luckily for me, I caught a break that very same weekend, and did not end up having to go back to Liza's home after all. A couple named Anthony and Monica, whom I had met at a function, called and said they had a job opening for an administrative clerk at the company they worked at. The position needed to be filled immediately and they asked if I was interested.

They also had an extra room in their house that I could rent. I jumped at the offer and moved in with them the next day. That was 4th November 1980 – I remember the day clearly because it happened to be the anniversary of the death of my husband. I started working for Executive Trading Company the day after that. Everyone there was very friendly, and it reminded me of Browns Group. I was so happy to have my first office job in the USA, and so grateful for the opportunity to work there.

As soon as I got my first paycheck, I opened my first checking and savings account at Security Pacific Bank at Western and Santa Monica. After all my expenses, I managed to save a few hundred dollars in those months. Before long I found myself my first apartment and moved out of Anthony and Monica's home.

It was a cozy, furnished, one bedroom apartment in Hollywood near Normandy and Fountain. Moving was

T e e r a

easy since I only had a few items of clothing and a TV that I was paying for on installments. Friends helped me by bringing their extra plates, pots and pans.

The freedom to have my own home after so many years was so liberating. I was on top of the world. I couldn't stop singing the song "Heaven." "I'm in heaven," I sang to myself as I unpacked my things.

I thought, "if Heaven is a place like this, I would be very happy to go there when the good Lord calls my name." I took the bus to work next day and smiled at each person that passed by, even strangers, just like I used to when I was a kid. Everything was perfect, and I was so hopeful about this new chapter in my life.

Three days after I had moved into my apartment, I was called in to speak with my bosses, Frank and Linda, while at work. I walked confidently down the long hallway; ready to tackle whatever task they had in store for me that day. Unfortunately Frank and Linda were not nearly as eager as I was when I stepped into their office. They asked me to sit down. They looked worried.

"We are so sorry Teera," Linda said, "but business is bad right now, very bad. We may have to close soon. At the very least we need to make some cutbacks. Since you were the last person to join our company, we are going to ask you to be the first one to leave."

My joy turned to panic.

"Linda, but how…but I…" I stuttered. "I just moved into my apartment!"

"Yes Teera," Linda said, "we know. We wish we didn't have to do this, but our hands are tied. If you'd like, you could move in with us. You could take over the house-keeping job until you find something better.

"Thank you Linda," I said, "but I already paid a deposit and a month's rent. I think I'll stay there until I figure out what to do next.

"We understand, Teera," Frank said. "But the offer still stands. Let us know when you go in for any job interviews. We're happy to give a good referral to anyone that asks for one!"

I thanked them, and quietly left the room.

The silence was overwhelming when I walked back to my seat. The rest of the staff came to my desk and tried to lift my spirits. They comforted me and assured me they'd look for work for me. Once again I said thank you, and fought the urge to lose my composure.

"I'll be alright," I added. "This isn't the end. I've gone through worse."

When I got home that gloomy evening it really did feel like the end of the world. "Why so many struggles, God?" I prayed, "Why so many tests?"

I called Cyril and he remained calm about the situation. He told me to pack up and come back to his house. I thanked him for the offer, but had I already paid rent on my new apartment and figured that it would be easier to stay in L.A. and find work there. I knew there were more opportunities in L.A. than there were in Lancaster.

My courage was shattered but I got up early the next morning and went job hunting until late in the evening. I was back to square one. I knocked on doors and dialed phone numbers that I found in the classified ads.

Before long, my spirits were raised when a few of my old co-workers from Executive Trading Company were able to get me an interview at a company called A-1 Mailing. Linda gave me an excellent recommendation and the owner was glad to hire me. It was good to know that my friends at ETC were still looking after me.

The new job was part-time and the pay was not enough to cover my expenses. My rent itself was $295. Then there was everything else: food, electricity, boarding fees for my boys back in Sri Lanka. On top of that, I had to try and find a way to save money for my children's passage. At four dollars an hour for three days of work, it was impossible to make ends meet.

I tried to be as thrifty as I could, but nevertheless my savings ran out in no time. I remember standing in the cashier's line at Hughes Market with twenty dollars in hand, adding up the price of my groceries and hoping that I had enough to cover the cost.

On my off days, I continued to walk the streets and scan the papers for work. I figured that if I had gotten this far, there was no reason that I couldn't go further. Determined to carve out a living for myself, there was nothing to stop me from trying to find my way. I kept my head down and put the time in, hoping and praying I would find myself a better job eventually. I had to. It was my only option.

After much searching, my prayers were finally answered. I found myself employed at the Los Angeles Medical Center by a Sri Lankan physician who went by the nickname Dr. J. A long time friend of Cyril's, Dr. J. took me in for an interview and reminisced with me about life back in Sri Lanka. I started in the mailroom. After a few months there, I was promoted and given the title: Head of the Purchasing Department.

It was refreshing to be able to work for a fellow immigrant that could empathize with the different challenges I was facing at the time. I had a lot of respect for Dr. J, and took pride in working for him. Seeing someone that had come as far as he did was a real inspiration for me.

The work was very rewarding and it felt good to have a job suited to my skills. In the morning I would water Dr. J's Green House that he kept on the rooftop of the building. From there I would look out and inhale the smoggy air under a perpetually sunny sky. I'd gaze out on the city in front of me and think about how far I was from home and how far I had come. Things were finally falling into place. I talked it over with Cyril and we began applying for visas for my kids.

That Christmas Eve, after work, I joined my office in attending evening mass. The service was long and we were all tired from a busy week. Apparently I had been standing too long because I fainted in the pews.

At first I was embarrassed, but the incident quickly turned into a good joke between my co-workers and me. A few of them even thanked me for fainting because it gave them an excuse to leave early.

The next day was my first Christmas in my apartment. I was all by myself. I spent most of my day on my couch, in the dark. I wondered what my children were doing. I wondered what everyone in my family was doing.

My neighbors noticed that that the lights were off, so they called me, but I didn't feel like answering the phone. When I didn't pick up, they came over and knocked on the door. It was the Sri Lankan couple that lived across from my apartment. I answered the door and they greeted me with glad tidings and a bottle of wine. We laughed and we celebrated, and I was very glad they came over. When they left, I fell asleep on the couch with my clothes still on.

The next day, a few of the kids in the building found a discarded tree in the trash. It was still fresh, so they pulled it out of the dumpster and came to my apartment looking to sell it to me for $10. They were so clever and insistent; I could not help but buy it from them.

I told them that I didn't want to put it up, but again, they insisted, so up it went. They even found some streamers and ornaments from around the building to decorate it. It looked like a real Christmas tree by the time they were done with it. And even though Christmas was over, I figured it was nice that I could have it through New Years at the very least.

While I was working and going to school, I managed to get a car. I nearly scared the life out of Cyril while he was teaching me how to drive on the right side of the road. It took me a long time to get used to it, and we often ended up heading straight into oncoming traffic.

Eventually I got the hang of it, and it was so liberating to be able to comfortably drive around Los Angeles. I could go anywhere I wanted to regardless of bus schedules or anyone else's agenda. It was a really big step forward for me, until, of course it wasn't.

That January I was driving back from work with one of the girls from the Medical Center. It was drizzling that day. I stopped for a red light at Wilshire and Westlake, when my car's engine sputtered out and died. I turned the key repeatedly, but the engine wouldn't start back up. The drivers stuck behind me started honking, and I panicked at all the noise.

I kept trying, and the other drivers kept honking. Finally, the engine turned over, but I was afraid that it would die again so I sunk my foot into the gas pedal and spun the steering wheel so that we could get out of the intersection. My car took off like a fighter jet, and I lost control immediately.

Amazingly, I missed the thick tree that was growing from the sidewalk, not to mention the few pedestrians that were smart enough to get out of the way. Instead, I drove right through a parking meter, over the sidewalk, and slammed my car into a storefront window. When the car stopped, a few metal beams and a 'For Lease' sign fell on the hood.

When the dust had settled, the two of us stumbled out of the car; we were both OK, and very thankful for it. It was a miracle that no one got hurt. After narrowly missing several pedestrians and a tree, I drove through a vacant storefront window that was located in between two busy tenants on either side. The car rested neatly inside the empty space as if it were parked in a garage.

I'm still grateful that no one was hurt that day. In a physical sense, the accident was nothing short of a miracle. Financially, however, I knew that the event would be a disaster because I was driving without insurance. I almost broke down as I stood next to my car, covered in glass. I thought I was going to be arrested when the police came. If I got arrested, I might never get to send for my children.

The police officer that came to the scene must have noticed how shaken I was. He showed me so much empathy and understanding. His kind words threw me off; I couldn't imagine such gentility from a police officer. He told me that he was so sorry he had to write a report on the incident.

The young officer's humility really put me at ease, and I was so relieved that I wasn't going to jail. Kind words can be short and easy to speak, but their echoes are truly endless. I never forgot that police officer's kindness, even though by now I am sure he has forgotten me.

I stopped driving for a while, at least until I could afford to buy insurance. My co-workers made fun of me at the office saying, "Teera doesn't believe in parking lots, she just drives right into the store!"

Everyone had a real good laugh about the accident, and with good reason. The whole thing was pretty ridiculous. But I wasn't laughing when legal notices and bills for damage started showing up in my mailbox. I couldn't afford the fines and damages associated with the accident, especially since I would have to pay out of pocket. Thinking that I had no other option, I ignored the collection notices as they continued to pile up at my door.

Before long, I forgot about the accident altogether. Months went by and my penalties piled up without me even thinking about it. Eventually I received a letter from the DMV saying that my license had been suspended. By that point, my legal fees and fines had amounted to just about five thousand dollars.

I didn't know what to do. I didn't have that much money, but I needed my license to get to work. I frantically asked friends and family for advice and found that my best option was to pay $1000 to an attorney and file for bankruptcy.

I got my license back, but it cost me in the end. With penalties, interest, and legal fees, I paid more money than I ever would have if I had just offered to make payments on my damages in the first place. I learned, the hard way, that there are no shortcuts; and that the best way to face your problems, is head on.

1982 and 1983 were both very big years for me. Soon after the fallout from my accident, I received word that the visas for my boys had been approved. Since Shirlene was safe with Sheila in Nigeria, Cyril and I figured that we would wait to send for her. That way we could put everything we had towards getting Jude and Damian out of Sri Lanka.

Getting the two of them here was a challenging proposition. The last thing we wanted was for Maxie to find out that Cyril and I had bought a flight for our son. He could do anything to Damian while I wasn't there.

We planned the trip under a veil of secrecy. Not even the boys were allowed to know that we had bought flights for them. The day of their departure, their aunt Margaret simply signed them out of school, told them to pack their things, and drove them to the airport. Neither of them knew where they were going until they got in the car.

Jude and Damian were in America with me the very next day. I still didn't believe they were really coming home to me. Even on the morning of their flight, on my way to the airport, I still couldn't believe it was happening. My eyes filled with tears as I watched Jude and Damian trudge sleepily through the terminal. They looked so much older. Jude had grown into a handsome young man, 17 years old at the time. Damian's limbs were long, his voice in transition, and his face still glowing like it had when he was a little boy; a young teenager at 13. He was growing up just like I imagined he would. I ran to grab the two of them and held on for as long as they would let me.

I joyously listened to my boys complain about the long flight as I whisked the two of them back to my cramped apartment. Just like Cyril did for me, I made them a genuine Sri Lankan meal when they got home from the airport. It was Damian's birthday that day. I made him a cake and a few kids that lived in the building joined us. We sang and laughed together like I had always hoped we would. That night I slept with a smile on my face knowing that my two sons were home safe with me.

The next morning I arose to the blissful sounds of Jude and Damian snoring peacefully in the next room. I quietly sat down at the kitchen table, sipped coffee and basked in freedom. An enormous hole in my soul had been filled, and it seemed as though I was about to burst with happiness.

Jude and Damian spent the next few days adjusting themselves to their new home. Damian was upbeat and excited for this new experience, but Jude was not. He was frustrated that we had to keep him in the dark about his departure; that he never got the chance to say goodbye to his friends.

He told me that he was going to save his money so that he could fly back to Sri Lanka as soon possible. I tried to reason with him, but of course, being a teenager, he wouldn't listen. I tried to tell him how I understood, how my father had shipped me off to go live with Sheila in Amparai for dating Sam. But for Jude, the words fell on deaf ears.

Jude didn't know it just yet, but it was a blessing having him with us. Damian still needed the influence of his older brother, now more than ever. He needed someone to look up to, someone that would love him and give him solid advice, and Jude was just that. I was so happy that the two of them were getting along. I could see my family coming together before my eyes and I thanked God for every minute of it.

I took time their first week to buy the two of them clothes and make sure that they had everything they needed. I enrolled Damian in school and Jude soon began taking classes at a technical college to become an X-Ray technician. In his spare time, Jude took up part time jobs to help support the family. He was an enormous help to all of us physically, emotionally, and yes, financially. I was impressed to see him take on so much responsibility.

With my two boys finally living happily with me, I began to hope that the day I saw Shirlene would not be too far off. That following year, in 1983, my prayers were answered in the form of an in-law's expired work visa. Sheila's husband was being forced to move from Nigeria. Instead of going back to Sri Lanka, Sheila wanted to come to California, and she was bringing Shirlene with her.

It didn't take long to get the paperwork together. As soon as Sheila could book their flights, the two of them were on a plane bound for Los Angeles. I'll never forget seeing my beautiful daughter at the airport as she bounced so carefree towards her family that missed her more than anything.

I was so happy that Sheila was letting me care for Shirlene again. Over the years, she had become reluctant to place Shirlene back in my care, and I understood where she was coming from. If anything I was grateful that someone like Sheila was caring for my daughter while I faced my demons. But after so much trying and so much painful learning, I had finally gotten my life back. I was safe and stable, free, but also ready to have my children come live with me in peace.

In time I would face further challenges as I attempted to stay connected to my children, who had learned to grow up without their mother. My relationship with each of them had indeed become fractured over the course of the many years where I had to spend time away from them. It was heartbreaking, the times that they wouldn't open up to me, when they wouldn't let me in. Through a lot of talking, a lot of listening, and a lot of praying we got through it, and today we are a tight-knit family.

I approached that next Christmas, with a renewed sense of fulfillment. With a full house, a good job, and food on the table, I felt accomplished and at peace. It was a feeling that at one time, I did not think was possible. With high spirits, I brought my children to the Medical Center's holiday party. The four of us took the opportunity to celebrate and look back on the events of that tremendous year.

The holiday party culminated in a ceremony where I was given an award for "Outstanding Contribution" to the Los Angeles Medical Center. The award, for me, was a total surprise. Dr. J, the staff and Cyril had all been in on it, and they did a good job of not spoiling the surprise. I didn't know what to say, I was so thrilled to be given the commendation.

I called my mother and sent copies of the award to my siblings and Sr. Finbarr back at the Welcome House. I wanted them to know that I was doing well, and that the sacrifices they had made for me had paid off.

I especially wanted my mother to know. To her, I was still her timid little girl. I was still her Bubby, her youngest child who still needed attention, who still needed love. I wanted her to know that I was able to make a life for myself in the U.S., that her little girl had grown up to become a proud woman with a good family. I wanted her to know that her work was done, and that she had done a fine job of raising me.

Life continued to pick up its pace as we headed into the New Year. The good times did not last forever, as I soon received word from back home that Mamma had passed away. I couldn't afford to go for her funeral, and the decision to stay home left me sleepless at night. I just wished I could have seen her one more time before she passed away. My mother was an enormous influence in every aspect of my life. She taught me how to be a woman, and in the process left a challenging example for me to follow.

In the weeks following my mother's passing, I began to hear the stories of how exactly it all happened. Margaret was there; she held my mother's hand while she closed her eyes. Even though she was sick, Margaret said Mamma's final hours were filled with the love of her family, and that she donned an expression of peace and relief when she finally allowed herself to let go.

It was my father who was hurt the most after my mother passed away. With his body failing him, and his wife no longer by his side, my father only lived a short while longer before he eventually gave himself up to God.

Pappa was very proud of his accomplishments. A talented architect, he felt very connected to the various projects he contributed to. His crowning achievement was the new altar for the Wadduwa church. His father, Abraham, was one of the founding members of that church and it meant so much to my pappa when they asked him to design and build it. As he was losing his sight at the time, my father knew that the altar would be his final contribution to the town he called home.

Pappa continued to maintain a respectable poise even in his later years. He rode his motorcycle until he was seventy, and even then, it was not his muscles, but his sight, that prevented him from getting back on the bike. He lived for another twenty-eight years, taking his final breath at 98 years old. Nothing could stand in the way of my father's indomitable will. As Margaret said over the phone when he passed, "he fought heroically right to the very end."

My parents were married for over sixty years. Devoted to each other for all sixty of those years, they were still very much in love with each other when they passed away. My father's anger hurt their relationship severely, but that was something he struggled with even into the latter part of his life. I often wonder how their marriage might have been different if my father had learned to control his emotions; I wonder how my family might have been different.

He once told me, "Bubby, don't ever forget that honesty is the true path to freedom." As hard as it has been to rationalize the sentiments of my father, his words still resonate with me. I tried not to lose sight of his words when he was living, and now that he's gone, I find that I can't bring myself to let go of them.

Maxie passed away some time later. He had gotten drunk and fallen down a staircase rendering him with head wounds and internal bleeding. He was taken to the hospital where he died few days later.

"He died the way he lived," Damian said when we both found out. "Dad never knew when to stop; he never knew when to say 'no.'"

Jude and Shirlene came by as soon as they heard the news. We went to church, lit candles, and prayed together as a family. Maxie adored Jude and Shirlene. From the moment we started seeing each other, Maxie was proud to tell the world that they were his children. He wanted to change their last names to Manatunge, but I declined. I admired him for wanting to be called a daddy. His willingness to embrace the title was one of the things that made it easy for me to overlook Maxie's imperfections.

During the beginning of our relationship Maxie's instability was easy to ignore because he offered me the security and human touch that I so desperately needed. In a time of despair and uncertainty, Maxie was my knight in shining armor, the one that saved me from my isolation.

As much as I thought that I should, I could never bring myself to hate Maxie. Maxie was one of the few people that took me in after Chandra's murder. Although he used me for everything I was worth, I opened up to him in the brief months where our relationship was still good. It seemed like we had a lot in common when we first met. He brought me out of the sorrow I was dwelling in, and convinced me to get my life back on track. He took me dancing and encouraged me to join the Browns Group netball team. He swept me off my feet, but to my great sadness those good times were short lived.

I still remember the night we won the baila competition at the Air Force dance. My Browns Group netball team had just won the finals that year. The celebrations went on the whole night, and so did the dancing competition. It wasn't until about 4:15 a.m. when we were tapped on our shoulders, and the MC announced us as the winners.

I often wondered how Maxie came to live as such a malignant person. It is my belief that no one is born a criminal. Much like me, Maxie had grown up with demons in his past that he had never learned to cope with.

He lost his mother when he was younger. While he was growing up his father tied him to a tree in front of their house, humiliated and beat him publicly. Maxie held on to this pain for the entirety of his life, attempting to blot it out with rage.

Never equipped with a sense of self-esteem or security, he never learned to use his many talents and brilliant intellect for anything good or legitimate. He had only been cheated and lied to while was growing up, so in turn that is how he learned to interact with people, and how he learned to make a living. He cheated and he lied, and never once thought about the damage that it would cause.

But the person that Maxie lied to the most was himself. Convinced that all this time he had been advancing, Maxie was left alone and in some ways helpless towards the end of his life. Having alienated almost every person that was once close to him, Maxie had run out of people that he could take advantage of. Once everyone else had already given up on him, he suddenly became the loser, the one who was no longer in control.

The words didn't sink in until years later, but Ranjani, Maxie's sister, once said, "Teera, you need to get away from him, or you too will die young like our mother did."

A few years prior to his death, I had received a letter from Maxie. It was the first and last word I would receive from him following my departure from Sri Lanka. In the letter he apologized for the things that he had done to me, and remarked on how despicable his behavior had been.

He sent his regards to the children and expressed the hope that one day he could make amends with me. He went on to explain about his new job in the Middle East and asked for me to send money to support him. Content with the apology I had received, I chose not to write back.

Against the wishes of my siblings, I requested that my brother Anthony attend Maxie's funeral. I asked him to bring flowers for me; Maxie would always come to my doorstep with flowers whenever he hurt me. It was a small gesture, and often times not enough, but flowers came to be something I remembered him by.

Shortly after Maxie's funeral, Cyril fell ill with cancer. I immediately began devoting a large portion of my time to being with him and assuring that he was comfortable. He had taken such good care of me along the way, I felt as though it was my duty to return the favor.

Some days I would spend at his home, and others he we would stay at mine. I remember one day, while he was resting at my home, following a treatment, he began commenting on how well my children had grown up.

He told me how glad he was that he sponsored our immigration, and that he was elated to see how close my family had become. He told me that he felt like God had called him to sponsor our immigration. The words meant a lot to me, coming from a man that outwardly did not believe in religion.

I still hold on to one of the birthday cards that Cyril gave me in his final year on earth. It read, "You touch others with God's love."

When I received word that Cyril's condition had taken a turn for the worst, I dropped everything I was doing and drove to him as fast as I could. I didn't know it when I pulled in the driveway, but I was too late.

It hurt that I never had a chance to properly say my goodbyes, but I think that's the way Cyril would have preferred it. He was never one for good byes. We left off on a good page, and I think that's exactly how he wanted it.

After the funeral his daughter Desiree called me aside. She said, "Aunt Teera, I figured you'd want to hold on to my dad's passport."

It was the same passport he used to make his one and only trip to Sri Lanka. Memories of that miraculous trip that brought the two of us together flooded my thoughts as I held the document. I felt so much stronger after she had given it to me. Good memories, I've come to learn, certainly have a way of keeping us alive.

In the wake of a season in my life filled with too many obituary notices, I took a break to slow down. Burnt out from the constant hustle of the city, I moved to a small house in Palmdale, one that was much closer to my kids, who by then, were living on their own.

It was there, in Palmdale, that the feeling really began to hit me. I had fewer responsibilities, fewer worries, and my days began to feel slow, stale even. My children had grown up and had moved on. It was an idea that I couldn't find the heart to comprehend, but for many reasons, it seemed as if my work was done. I had conquered my demons, found a safe home, and reunited my family. All the pieces had come together. What else could I do?

I knew there had to be more. I kept waking up and thinking to myself, "what is my next assignment? What is it that God wants me to do?"

Throughout my life I had always struggled under the weight of overbearing circumstances. The pain has made me stronger, and I take pride in the fact that I have gracefully lived through so much. I had always been charitable to those that needed help, but I also had never taken the time to actively give back.

I especially felt as though I was indebted to all those who had helped me on the way. I had only taken from the kindness of those around me over the years. It was not as though I had lived selfishly, but until then, I had never been in any sort of position to give back.

I remember the revelation coming to me as I sat down in Church one afternoon to light a candle. Reflecting in silence, I began to think all those to whom I owe my gratitude. A lot of names came to mind; a lot of friends and a lot of family; a lot of people who had encouraged me, or fed me, or cared for my children or offered me shelter. I thought about all of these angels that had, at one time or another, helped save me. The list was endless, but the more that I thought about it, the more that one name in particular continued to stand out to me.

The Welcome House needed me more than anyone did. Their whole operation depends on the generosity of those who are in a position to give. Having found my success in America, I realized it was now my calling to give back to the sisters that helped me get on my feet. The sisters at the Welcome House saved my life. And it was about time that I gave back for the unconditional support they had given me.

It began with a simple donation of $150, which I wired to the Welcome House after excitedly reaching my old friend Sister Joan on the phone. She said that the convent had fallen on hard times in the past few years and that money was especially tight for them. The building was beginning to fall into disrepair and some weeks the nuns were having trouble ensuring that the women and children they looked after were all properly fed.

Sister Finbarr had passed away a few years before at the age of 93. I learned about it when I called Sister Joan to make my donation. I know she was missed at the Welcome House. I felt as though I was making my donation in her honor.

It felt good to make a difference, and I didn't want to stop there. I got out my pen and wrote letters to every single friend or family member that I could think of. I asked them to open their hearts and make a similar contribution to an organization that was really helping people. I explained to them how much the Welcome House meant to me and shared with them my hopes of keeping the convent open for years to come.

The project ended up costing the better part of a week, not to mention that some money had to be set aside for postage, printing, and stationery. I crossed my fingers and dropped my stack of letters in the mail, hoping that my friends and family would understand what a difference they could make with their contributions. The responses came in slow at first, but as people caught on, my mailbox began filling with pledges. Some donations were big, some were small, and some came from people that I had not had any contact with in decades.

Sister Joan nearly fainted when I told her the news, and after the success of our first appeal, I made a pledge to continue my efforts as long as I possibly could. Since then, I send out the same appeal, every year at Christmas time. Every year my friends and family contribute. And every December the Welcome House faces the coming year with a little bit more money, and a renewed sense of hope.

After nearly giving up so many times, I had finally escaped my troubles and grew strong enough to give back. I was nobody's victim. I had a strong heart and a stoic sense of duty. Even though I had already gone through much, I realized that I still had a lot more living left to do.

Nearly four decades later, I still miss my husband, my Chandra. Throughout everything I have been through, I never let go of his memory; not when I left Sri Lanka, not even when I found myself engaged to a new man. Chandra was my soul mate and I can see so much of him in my eldest son. I often pray that he be with me, and at times, I know that he is.

I had never attained closure. In time I came to grow accustomed to the idea of Chandra's absence. His not being there was something that I came to accept. The night of his murder, however, the incident, his family, all of the details of that event tugged at me still. My husband's killer was never identified, and consequently never brought to justice.

I finally felt compelled to do something, and decided that I needed to reach out to someone that I knew from that time in my life. Thinking back to all the people that I was in contact with back then, one person that stood out was Silva's cousin Kumara.

Kumara had warned me about the greed and envy of Chandra's mother and sister. He was the only one of Chandra's cousins that I trusted after the murder, and I could never thank him enough for standing by me back then.

Unsure of his address, I hesitantly sent Kumara a letter thanking him and asking for an update on the family. Surprisingly, I heard back from him only a week or so later. Much had changed since the last time I found myself in Dodanduwa. Most of the family had passed on, and life had become very quiet.

Sirimathi and Somapala were living in the beach house. The two had turned the residence into a guesthouse for tourists. Apparently they were making a pretty good living charging inflated prices to pale-skinned visitors that don't know any better.

The sign out front bearing the name "Chitral" was thrown in the garbage years ago. Gunapala lives a few houses from Sirimathi and Somapala. Some years prior, the two had adopted one of Gunapala's daughters. Gunapala was later elected as a Justice of Peace in Dodanduwa, and has since been using his power to carry out bloody vendettas throughout town.

I still wonder if that house was worth the life of my husband. I wonder if Sirimathi and Somapala made enough money to compensate for the guilt they carry knowing they had arranged for his murder. We never wanted the house in the first place, and if Chandra's sister and mother wished to negotiate peacefully for it, he might have given it up to them. There was never any need for bloodshed. That property was never worth ruining our lives over.

I wrote back to Kumara, thanking him for his letter. Sadly, he fell ill and passed away before my words had the chance to reach him. That letter I received from Kumara was the last contact I would ever receive from him, and no doubt the last opportunity I would have to attain the closure that I needed. I know who did it, I know who paid to have it done, and I know why they did it. I have come to accept my husband's murder, I've learned to live with my scars, and I no longer have nightmares about waking up to the sound of sharpened metal against bone. It is all in the past now.

About the same time that Kumara passed away, I received word that my brother Marcus had also fallen ill. When I received word, I thought about how much it would cost, and how much it would mean for me to go back. I thought about how I missed my parents' funerals, and two of my brothers' funerals, and couldn't stand the idea of missing any more. Now that I could afford it, and now that I knew I was ready, I booked tickets and made plans for Damian and me to go back to Sri Lanka.

Upon arrival, we were all relieved to find Marcus pulling through. We attended a service to give thanks for his good health, and afterwards were left with a few extra days that had originally been set aside for attending to Marcus' bedside. With my free time, I decided to leave for Dodanduwa to attend an almsgiving service for Kumara. Margaret, her son Gaya, and Damian came along with me.

Back in Dodanduwa for my first visit in over 39 years, I stepped through town allowing myself to be swept away by memories of my haunted past. It all came back to me: the dinners with the uncles, Sirimathi's wedding, the sound of Chandra's skin slapping on our bedroom floor. I thought about returning to the beachside house. It was an idea that Chandra's relatives encouraged at the service. I was reluctant at first, but deep down, I knew that going back there was something that I had to do.

Dodanduwa had changed a lot, so finding the house proved to be somewhat difficult. Eventually the streets took a familiar turn and my stomach dropped as I saw the structure materializing in the distance. The front of the house was secured with a tall, metal fence that surrounded the compound. The fence created an intimidating barrier of rusted steel between the home and the outside world.

Beyond the fence the house looked more or less the same from outside. The inside, however, had been rebuilt to accommodate tourists. I arrived there unannounced and unsure if anyone would even be home. I gathered my courage, marched through the gate and approached the door where a feeble man with a blank expression greeted me as a stranger.

"Hello," I said politely. "I'm sorry, but what is your name? Who are you?"

Slightly confused, the man answered, "Somapala, I'm Somapala… who are you?"

"Somapala, it's Teera," I said with a smile. Somapala's expression changed and his voice began to tremble.

"Teera," he said, "would you like to come inside?"

I stepped lightly through the threshold so as not to disturb anyone or anything around me. I wanted to be sure that I maintained my composure. I was by no means in the company of friends in this house.

"Where's Sirimathi?" I asked as she quietly crept into the living room behind me. I turned around and the two of us froze as our eyes met.

"Teera," Sirimathi said, "When did you get here?"

"I came from Kumara's almsgiving," I said cautiously.

"How did you know he was dead?" Sirimathi asked as if that was privileged information.

196

"Kumara and I kept in touch. I was in Sri Lanka to visit my brother and thought I might pay my respects while I'm here," I said.

"Well, um, Teera," Somapala offered. "Would you like me to show you the rest of the house?"

"No thank you," I said politely. "But I would like to see the backyard."

As we exited out the back of the house, the familiar scent of salty wind brushed briskly against my face. Past the fence surrounding the backyard you could still see the water and the overturned boats along the shore. The three of us made small talk. After a few minutes, Sirimathi began to feel more comfortable and asked, "why haven't you kept in touch with us?"

I was stunned by the question. Words of rage bubbled up inside of me. "Well, after everything that had happened," I said.

Before I let myself go on, I chose to stop. She wasn't worth it. And my anger would have accomplished nothing. Besides, so long as I take the higher road, she can't touch me. Sirimathi and I stared blankly at each other as the conversation trailed off.

She asked me how the children were doing. I asked her about Chandra's parents. They had both passed on some years before.

"Well Teera," Somapala said, "do you want to come inside? Are you thirsty? Can we get you anything?"

I wouldn't have been able to stomach the water from their tap. Instead I told Somapala that I had already eaten and made my departure as quickly as possible. We approached the front door where Somapala asked for my address so that we could keep in touch. His hand shook as he wrote down my information.

Sirimathi's face carried no remorse or guilt. As I hugged her before leaving, I finally came to accept the fact that she never would own up to her crimes. I don't understand how someone could be so callous, but there are many things about that woman and about that family that I will never understand.

I was done being angry with them for what they had done to us. There was nothing that I could extract from them that would erase my pain or bring back my husband. The only thing left to do was to learn to let go. Having been back to the house that day, I finally realized that I was ready to forgive them.

A few days after my visit to Dodanduwa, I received a phone call from Sister Immaculate at the Welcome House. "Teera," she said. "I heard you were in Sri Lanka, when are you coming to visit your home?"

Sister Immaculate greeted me at the convent with open arms. There was a lunch prepared for my visit, and I excitedly sat down with everyone. We caught up on events, and I told them stories about the U.S. Sister Immaculate had big plans for expanding the Welcome House and I was anxious to offer my assistance. She talked of beginning programs for the orphaned children of Sri Lanka's prison inmates. I figured that with enough funding we would be able to provide the resources necessary for these children to meet their educational requirements.

As soon as I mentioned the idea of supporting these children in school, the sisters began talking about a scholarship fund and I promised to keep sending my support from the United States. Before I left, Sister Immaculate reminded me that as long as the Welcome House is there, I would always have a home in Sri Lanka.

I took the train to Wadduwa on the last day of my trip. The old market where I stopped to buy bananas and papayas still stood right across from the railway station. Behind me I could hear the serendipitously stunning voice of a beggar that was singing for spare change. He sat with his toothless wife as she hummed along to the simple tunes I remembered from my childhood.

Past the train station I walked down the road to gaze upon the church where my father made his final contribution to the town he had spent his life in. Beyond the church is the school where he gave free architectural lessons to underprivileged students.

I stopped in to the church to meet the current pastor. I told him how my father had designed the altar when the church was rebuilt. The priest went into his office and brought me a magazine printed to celebrate the church's 125th Jubilee. In the magazine was a page with a list of people who had contributed to the church over the years. I was so proud to read my father's name in that list.

A stone's throw from the beach, the house I grew up in still stands, right where it always had. The sign that reads "Sea Breeze" is still posted out front, even though a different family lives there now. Past my house I stepped barefoot on the beach where I sat quietly on the hull of an overturned boat. I filled my lungs with sea air and greeted the setting sun.

I gazed out on the beach that I could once call my own, a beach that now belongs to the next generation of young children running to the seashore on Sundays. And from what I understand, the kids still scavenge for the loose fish that flop out of the fishing nets. It was a beautiful place for me to grow up and I can only hope that the kids living there now will feel the same way.

Walking away from the beach I could hear the echoes of the fisherman singing the same old song while they dragged in their nets. "Odellai, ellaiya!" they chanted as I trudged through thick sand towards the sound of a passing train whistle.

It was Christmas time in Sri Lanka, and I couldn't help but be whisked back to my childhood. My heart ached as I remembered how I used to spend New Year's Eve with my family as a little girl. I remembered how much it meant to us, and how happy we were as a family. Those joyous nights where we danced and sang while my brothers played guitar and accordion were so far in the past, it was hard to believe they even happened.

During Christmas, the village would come alive with people making preparations for the holiday. In the evenings children would skip about the street singing Christmas carols in the twilight hours. Down the way the church would have a long line for the confessional, and every Christmas Eve the choir would bring the packed congregation to tears with their on point rendition of 'Adeste Fideles.'

I went to main street Colombo to browse through the shops just like Sheila and I had done when we were younger. On the way back I stopped by the Memorial Hall at Independence Square where every February 4th we would celebrate Sri Lanka's independence day. I thought about the time I led the Good Shepherd Convent's marching band to the music of the Colonel Bogey March from the movie "Bridge on the River Kwai". It felt like yesterday that I carried the school flag. I waved it with so much enthusiasm and pride.

Later, I went back to the Wadduwa church during a service. I sat in the back. The pews smelled just like they did when I was little. It warmed my heart to see that everyone now had a bench, and that the poorer parishioners didn't have to stand in the back. I thanked God for all that he has given me and prayed he would continue to guide me in my final years.

It had been so long since I wept in the Wadduwa church. I was only a girl the last time that I had done it. I still remember how my teardrops looked as they dried on the stone floor. Quietly, I left that service with a smile on my face, proud of how far I had come since then.

I flew back to the US some time after Christmas. Without the songs of my brothers, the evening seemed dull. My life in Sri Lanka had gone on without me. I had done what I had come there to do, and it was time for me to go back to where I now belonged.

Before leaving, I made one final trip to Mt. Lavinia beach, making sure that I brought a pocketful of coins for the children that I knew would be playing along the water. Walking past the slow, rolling waves, I found a little boy about eight or nine years old, washing his face in a bucket of water. The boy was with his mother, a young woman wearing an old sari that looked over him from the trees that backed up to the sand.

I waved to the boy but he was reluctant to come towards me. I looked up and met eyes with the mother who gave the boy a gesture of approval. When the little boy came closer to me, I grabbed the coins from my pocket and held out my hand. He excitedly put both his hands together to make a little tray. I giggled to myself as I dumped the whole heap of coins into his tiny palms. The little boy's face lit up. He took the coins and skipped away. I turned around and walked back down the beach towards my hotel. Behind me I heard him calling his mother over so that he could show her.

Clouds were gathering that afternoon, the air grew thick and I felt the familiar plop of water droplets on the top of my head. I slowed my pace and looked up to feel the raindrops of my home country beating down on my eyelids. Quietly I hummed the tune to "Singing in the Rain" as my clothes took on the familiar feeling of being soaked and heavy in a warm tropical downpour.

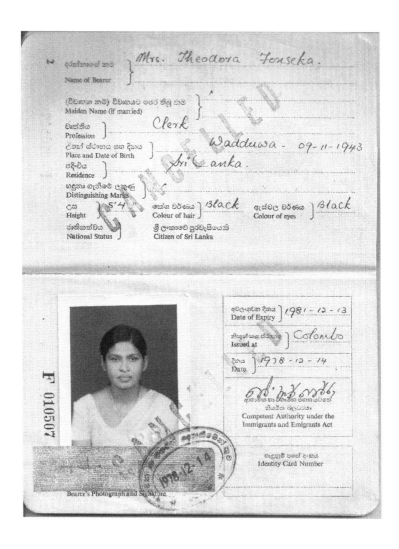

Teera

This picture was taken just after Christmas in 1981. That tree behind me is the tree that the neighborhood kids pulled out of the dumpster and decorated for me. They had so much fun dressing the tree up, they even hung an ornament on me!

My kids and I. Jude, Shirlene and Damian
at Shirlene's wedding in 2008.

ACKNOWLEDGEMENTS

We would like to send our heart felt thanks to all the people who lent their good wishes, encouragement and support for this book; for giving us ideas and enthusiasm to help its message reach as many readers as possible.

Teera's Acknowledgements:

Special thanks to Fr. Tom Allender S.J., Sr. Immaculate de Alwis, Sr. Jacintha Silva, Indu Bandara, Denis Silver, Arthur Jayasundera, Dinuli Senarathe, Kate Peris, Rick Rofman, Crown Bookstore, David Crockett, Silvia Cary, Dr. Walter Jayasingha, and all the friends and family who have continuously supported me with my fund raising efforts for the Welcome House in Sri Lanka, especially Indu Upsena for helping create their website.

And to: Dr. P. A. Lucero, Dr. Merlie Ocampo, Albert Sormanti, Aeshea & Dr. Walter Jayasinghe, Kiran & Anil Heteshi, Leo Rendon, Dr. Gracia Lewis, Janice and Denis Silver, Samira, Catherine, and Joeline Saleh, Sumudu &

Prasanna Silva, Luxshmi de Silva, Ulric J Patillo, Dave Drake, Felicia & Noel Pieris, Vivian Gray & Adrian Jayasinghe, Rachel Mayoral, Rachel Chargoy, Herbert Oorloff, Michel Oorloff, Preethi & Nanda Alagiyawanna, Sylvia Munoz, Patricia Barrow, Audrey & Rienzie Pinder, Shirani &Tyrone Stanislaus, Neela & Ranjith Silva, Fr. Cyprin G. Carlo, Mugo Muchiri, Dr. Geoffrey R. Keys, Dr. V. Pillai, MD Stella Jayasinghe, Indu Upasena, Dina & Raymond Levy, Carlyle Weinman, Ida & Mario Rodriguez, Grace and Jerome Holmes, Veronica Ruiz, Rebecca Laitaino, Dalrin Senaratne, Vicky Castaneda, Liliana Ordonez, Veronica & Christi Ignacius, Corrine & Tony Peterez, Lilamani & Mohan Perera, Romina and Leonard Jurie, Richard Jurie, Bernie & Ed Perera, Rudi La Vecchia, Ronald Martinez, Shana and Shami Wijeratne, Sherine Ganegoda, Rosemary Ashborne, Linda and Joseph Santiago, Nony Mazumder, Maritza Ponce, Mohamed J. Virani, Chatur Patel, Joe Emmanuel, Nira Emmanuel, Chris & Lucky Wickramasinghe, Fran, & Jeganathan, Ruby Velazquez, Jenny Avilez, Mirium Valasquez, Elba Jauregui, Gloria Munoz. My children. My son-in-law Gary Bjorling, grandchildren Jasmine, Jessica, Naomi, & Dominique.

Pat's Acknowledgements:

Tom Allender, Tim Meissner, Mary Meissner, Bryan, Kevin, Mikey, The Meissner sister(s), The Three Amigos, Yogi The Bear, Teera, Damian, Jude, Shirlene, Tigger, Rick Rofman, Mahlena Rae Johnson, Charles Fiore, Greg

Pierce, Justin Manzano, Ryan Cavalier, Justine Ciarrocchi, Liam Satre-Meloy, Gabe Polsky, Kate Peris, Gail Wronsky, Barry Schwartz, Michael Datcher, Shane Baker, Logan O'Brien, Numair Faraz, Abby Pierce, Nick Vitale, Adam Finer, Intelligentsia Venice, Jade Estrada, Allan Braun, Sean Gaynor, Long Nguyen and Ryan Conroy…you know, your book…

A NOTE ABOUT THE WELCOME HOUSE

From: Teera de Fonseka

It did not occur to me for a long time, that I could be the bearer of hope for the Welcome House in Sri Lanka. I was not quite sure what to do when I first heard the calling, so I did what I could to help keep their doors open. For the last 15 years I have tried to help in any way that I can, but I've always known that even my best is not enough. There is always more that can be done. Like Mother Teresa once said, "we cannot do great things on this earth, only small things with great love"

It takes a special person to give a helping hand when it is so easy to look the other way. I encourage you to be that special person and help give aid to the charity that saved my life. Your donations help provide basic necessities for the convent such as food and medicine. Your support for the Welcome House allows the nuns there to dedicate their time to counseling, healing and providing spiritual guidance for its residents. Your gift will also help promote the Welcome House's program to support and provide scholarships for the orphaned children of prison inmates that live in Sri Lanka.

I experienced first-hand all the wonderful work that the Welcome House is doing to help these women and children in distress. It did not matter that I was a total stranger to them. To the sisters at the Welcome House, I was seen as 'a person worth more than the whole world,' as their saintly founders had taught them to. It is an awesome privilege to be able to give back, and I pray that you will share in the joy and love that can come from your generosity.

Please help me support the Welcome House, so that they can help give a second chance at life to the women and children that need them so desperately, just like I did.

Sincerely,

Teera

The Good Shepherd Welcome House
www.welcomehousesrilanka.org

ABOUT TEERA DE FONSEKA

By: Pat Meissner

Teera de Fonseka is a mother, a grandmother, and a writer living in Los Angeles, California. In her free time she enjoys reading, writing and walking her dog, Tigger. Writing especially has become a hobby for Teera in recent years, as she has worked to publish her memoirs. She loves to spend her days, as she puts it, "writing her heart out."

Writing has brought Teera a great deal of peace and she wants to encourage others to write their hearts out too. She hopes that her story can touch and inspire others. After having had a chance to tell her tale, Teera wants to keep helping people. She finds inspiration in the talent that she sees in the people around her. She wants to encourage these people to do everything that they can with their talents, to live up to their potential and to trust in God's plan for them.

On a personal note, Teera is one of the most remarkable people that I have ever met. She has lived through more than any person that I have known, she has lost more than any person that I have known, and yet she is more grateful, generous, hopeful, and enthusiastic than I can even begin to articulate. That sweet little Sri Lankan lady has become my third grandma over the course of these past 4+ years, and I am so grateful that she has trusted me with her memoirs.

There is no one that encouraged me more, while working on this project, than Teera did. Even at the times where I doubted myself, Teera never gave up on me, and she still won't. She believed in me, and I in turn believe in her, and her story. I believe that Teera's life story needed to be told, that its message needed to reach as many people as it possibly could. Teera's story is one that deserved to be presented with great care, and I can only hope that I have done it justice.

ABOUT PAT MEISSNER

By: *Teera de Fonseka*

Patrick is young but has the gentleness and presence of an older person. His smile is warm and his concentration is inspiring. Often I felt like I was working with a much older gentleman who had been here lot longer than I have. He is brilliant, ambitious, smart, and witty. He speaks only when it is necessary, and is always eager to listen.

He is one of the best writers of the younger generation who can illuminate the drama and complexity of life with compassion, humor, and honesty. He is a rising star, and fits in anywhere. It doesn't matter where he is, or whom he is with, he adapts and always stays grounded.

We learned so much from each other and I found him to be a kid of integrity. To my amazement he turned out to be a remarkable young man who doesn't seem to have the need to impress anyone, and is comfortable in his own skin. On the weekends he is either writing or surfing. I call him a 'soul writer' and a 'solo surfer.'

When I heard his voice on the phone for the first time, I got the impression he was an older person with a lot of experience. Then the day he came to my doorstep, I was surprised to meet a cute adorable kid with the shining smile of a sixteen year old. At the time he was 22.

For a moment I doubted his ability to understand the story of a woman from a country like Sri Lanka, with an enormous age and culture gap. But I had confidence that Fr. Tom Allender would not have introduced Patrick to me unless he was sure of him. Tom told me that Pat had recently graduated from Loyola Marymount University, and that he was a "good kid."

It took longer than both of us expected to present my story. Patrick and I had our ups and downs, but we put our trust in each other, and never hesitated to clear up our misunderstandings through communication. We were always pleased with the results whenever we had to talk through the certain challenges we faced along the way. It has indeed been a long road.

Sometimes he became the detective, and came up with questions that made me go back to those trying times. He left no stone unturned to help make sense of the trials and tragedies that took place during my long battle.

Other times he became my therapist, and over time I learned that he is a peacemaker. We teamed up and worked long hours and days, which also became a part of my healing journey.

Our commitment to this project required patience, understanding and sacrifice. It has been a humbling and gratifying experience. I am excited and feel privileged to present my inspirational story to the world with Patrick Timothy Meissner, whom I sincerely believe is a rare gem of the younger generation, and beat the odds with flying colors.

May he be graced to find a silver lining of hope in the back of every dark cloud that may cross his path, just like I did.

In God's love,

Teera

Made in the USA
Columbia, SC
03 January 2020